TALKING ABOUT CULTS

GEORGE H. SHRIVER

LECTURE SERIES IN

RELIGION IN

AMERICAN HISTORY

NO. 11

TALKING ABOUT CULTS

ABUSE AND THE STUDY OF NEW RELIGIOUS MOVEMENTS

Ann Gleig

THE UNIVERSITY OF GEORGIA PRESS
Athens

Athens, Georgia 30602
www.ugapress.org

Set in 11/15 Adobe Caslon Pro by Rebecca A. Norton

Printed digitally

EU Authorized Representative
Easy Access System Europe—Mustamäe tee 50, 10621 Tallinn, Estonia, gpsr.requests@easproject.com

Library of Congress Cataloging-in-Publication Data

Names: Gleig, Ann author
Title: Talking about cults : abuse and the study of new religious movements / Ann Gleig.
Description: Athens : The University of Georgia Press, 2026. | Series: George H. Shriver Lecture Series in Religion in American History ; No. 11 | Includes bibliographical references and index.
Identifiers: LCCN 2026015198 | ISBN 9780820377896 hardback | ISBN 9780820377902 paperback | ISBN 9780820377919 epub | ISBN 9780820377926 pdf
Subjects: LCSH: Buddhism and social problems—United States—History | Buddhism—Social aspects—United States—History | Women—Religious aspects—Buddhism—History
Classification: LCC BQ734 .G54 2026 | DDC 294.30973—dc23/eng/20260520
LC record available at https://lccn.loc.gov/2026015198

CONTENTS

FOREWORD

The present volume presents in somewhat expanded form the George H. Shriver Lectures: Religion in American History delivered at Stetson University on March 25–26, 2025. Sponsored by the Department of Religious Studies and the Department of History, this biannual lecture series dates from the year 2000 and was endowed by the late Dr. George H. Shriver, Professor of History Emeritus at Georgia Southern University and an alumnus of Stetson University. As indicated by the title, the lecture series's focus is American religious history, broadly construed, and it has included lectures on topics from the faith of U.S. presidents to debates surrounding evolution in our culture wars to American Judaism, American Islam, and African American religion. As proud as we are of our past lectures, we were excited to move beyond the Abrahamic traditions with our twelfth Shriver lecturer, Dr. Ann Gleig, Associate Professor of Religion and Cultural Studies at the University of Central Florida, whose lectures were based on her ethnographic fieldwork with survivors of sexual abuse in American Buddhist communities.

As mentioned above, the present book both includes and expands on those lectures. Gleig begins by drawing our attention to the ways survivors of sexual abuse in American Buddhist communities have used cult discourse to describe their abuse. She then provides a short history of cult discourse, including both its weaponization against minority religions as well as the subsequent critique of that weaponization by some scholars of new religious movements (NRMs). Gleig observes, however, that along with these often legitimate critical interventions came the dismissal of survivors who employed cult discourse, which in turn led to the downplaying or even rejection of their accounts of sexual abuse. Drawing on her own ethnography of survivors of sexual abuse in Buddhist "convert" communities, she argues for a survivor-centered approach that takes the use of cult discourse by ex-members seriously. In doing so, she finds that her approach aligns with the work of other feminist scholars of NRMs. As Gleig notes, the consensus approach to cult discourse taken by scholars of NRMs has failed to give these survivors' voices their proper due. In light of her research as well as that of a growing number of scholars willing to challenge this consensus view, Gleig recommends the following as necessary corrections to reorient scholarship on abuse and cult discourse in NRMs: taking survivors of abuse in NRMs seriously as epistemological sources, acknowledging shifts within cult discourse and demographics, replacing predetermined theoretical frameworks with more empirically based understandings of power, and situating abuse in NRMs in the wider context of abuse in religion.

The lectures given by Dr. Gleig, and the present chapters in this book, stand as vitally important contributions to the relatively new field of religion and sexual abuse. I am grateful to Dr. Gleig for sharing not only her research but also her time with Stetson faculty and students; it was an absolute pleasure to host her.

I would like to take a moment to thank a few of the people without whom this lecture series would not be possible, especially the late Dr. George H. Shriver; this series continues to serve as a testimony to his generosity and intellectual curiosity. I would also like to extend my thanks to Dr. Emily Mieras, Associate Professor of History and American Studies, for her assistance as a member of the Shriver Lectures Committee. As always, administrative support provided by Ms. Lisa Guenther proved to be crucial to our success as Dr. Gleig's host. Finally, I express my deep appreciation to the University of Georgia Press, and especially Beth Snead, for the publication of these lectures.

Sam Houston, Chair
George H. Shriver Lectures Committee
Stetson University

ACKNOWLEDGMENTS

As I note in multiple places, this book is a spin-off project from a larger collaborative research project undertaken with Buddhist studies scholar Amy Langenberg on Buddhism and sexual abuse. In our cowritten book, we argue that the field of Buddhist studies has not paid sufficient attention to the issue of sexual abuse in Buddhism and that it needs to take survivors of abuse in Buddhist contexts more seriously as epistemological subjects. I am very grateful to Amy for generously allowing me to extend some of the insights from our collaborative research to the field of new religious movements. At the same time, any shortcomings of these lectures are entirely my responsibility. I am very grateful to all of the members of the Heartwood Connecting Survivors of Guru and Teacher Abuse group who participated in this study.

These lectures are a critique of the way that abuse allegations, ex-members, and the use of cult discourse have been treated by what I call the "consensus" approach in the academic field of new religious movements (NRM). I am indebted to the scholars who pointed out many of the problems around the treatment of abuse in NRM scholarship before me and particularly to feminist scholars of religion, at the forefront of whom is Janet Liebman Jacobs.

I am grateful for conversation and feedback from Marion Goldman, Anna Halafoff, Sarah-Jane Page, Phillip Lucas, Aled

Thomas, Philip Deslippe, Wendy Dossett, Claire Alison Hams, Sarah Harvey, Sarah Jacoby, Amelia Wood, Dana Logan, Yehudis Fletcher, Susannah Crockford, Matthew Remski, Tenzin Peljor, Nancy Floy, Rachel Montgomery, and Justin Rezzonico. I am also grateful to all the members of the former Jehovah's Witnesses reading group that I was invited to attend. Hearing their experiences helped me understand the challenges ex-members face in multiple contexts, including academia.

I also respect the scholarship by Catherine Wessinger and Rebecca Moore that shows the ways that abuse allegations and cult discourse have been weaponized to cause harm against members of minority religion. Their research is essential, and I do not see this book as replacing such scholarship but rather as expanding the field to better address abuse and harm *within* as well as *against* new religious movements.

I am a grateful recipient of the Gloria Anzaldúa Research Excellence Award from the Women's and Gender Studies Department at the University of Central Florida, which provided partial funding for this project. I owe the biggest thank-you to Sam Houston and Christopher Bell for their invitation to deliver the 2025 Shriver Lectures at Stetson University. It was such an honor to follow in the footsteps of esteemed previous Shriver Lecture speakers, and it was a real treat to spend time with the religious studies faculty and students at Stetson University.

I am grateful and indebted to Jeanine Viau, my colleague and partner. Jeanine has spent many hours talking through these issues with me, and her questions and insights were crucial in helping me to gain clarity on what I was arguing and why I was arguing it. She carefully read and incisively commented on multiple versions of the lectures that became this book. This work is dedicated to her.

TALKING ABOUT CULTS

CHAPTER 1

"I Know It's a Politically Incorrect Term, but I Was in a Cult"

Revisiting the Cult Wars

On September 11, 2024, Justin Whitaker, a journalist for the international online magazine *Buddhistdoor Global*, posted an article he described as a "difficult but necessary read" on his public Facebook page.[1] Written by Be Scofield, who describes herself as a "prominent cult reporter," it was titled "Secrets of Shambhala: In Pema Chodron's Shadow," with the subheading "Top Secret Texts Reveal the Cult-Like Inner Workings of Shambhala's Buddhism."[2] In the article, Scofield examines intergenerational sexual abuse and institutional complicity in the Shambhala Buddhism community through a cultic studies framework. She identifies many examples of cult characteristics—such as sexual abuse, labor exploitation, "an in-group and out-group," "a cult of personality," "a culture of denial, codependency and obfuscation," "deception," and "insular beliefs"—and concludes that Shambhala functioned as "military-themed Buddhist sex cult."

Whitaker's post generated 142 heated responses from academics, survivors, journalists, Buddhists, and former Buddhists. While he was thanked profusely by those identifying as survivors or allies of survivors of abuse in Buddhist contexts, Buddhist studies scholar Robert Mayer raised questions about the legitimacy of the testimonies contained in the article. He asked, "As an academic, my first question is, precisely which of these stories can one believe, and which ones are dubious, in a journalistic account where the author clearly has a vested interest in sensationalizing."[3] Another participant critiqued what she saw as Mayer's redirection of focus from accounts of abuse to the quality of the journalism that reported the abuse.[4] As she put it, "[It's] interesting that the 'academic' perspective goes after the journalist instead of spending time researching the topic." Whitaker, who has a PhD in Buddhist ethics, also named the perceived dichotomy between academia and sensationalist journalism as "an unfortunate misdirection" and tried to return attention to the factually documented case of abuse within Shambhala.[5] The debate over academic versus journalistic coverage raged on, however, with some particularly significant contributions coming from Tenzin Peljor, a German Tibetan Buddhist monk who hosts the popular blog *Tibetan Buddhism—Struggling with Diffi-Cult Issues*.[6] Many articles on Peljor's website draw on cult discourse as an interpretive framework to identify and explain abuse in Buddhism. Peljor first expressed his appreciation for Scofield and other journalists reporting on abuse. In his words, "As a survivor of cults and being a friend and a supporter for survivors of cults and sexual abuse survivors, I applaud and thank all of the journalists who have given us a voice." He contrasted journalists' support for survivors with academics' treatment of them, saying, "Academics have ignored our plight over decades. Our stories and what we have experienced has been [too] 'dirty' to deal with in the 'pure' 'academic world'—this is at least my feeling and my observation."[7]

Peljor's point was echoed by many on the discussion thread, who complained not only that academics had ignored abuse in "Buddhist cults" but that they had actually enabled it. As Kevin Knox put it, scholars had failed to report on abuse in Buddhist communities and "through such avoidance, have arguably been complicit in allowing such cults to continue to flourish and present themselves as legitimate religious institutions."[8] This pushback was somewhat unfair to Mayer, who himself acknowledged in the discussion that there were "cult like distortions" within Shambhala Buddhism.[9] His critique of sensationalist journalism, however, had unleashed a torrent of hurt, frustration, anger, and resistance from survivors over how academics have responded to their stories of abuse within what they identify as Buddhist cults.[10] I followed and participated in this Facebook discussion with great interest.[11] I had just finished a collaborative book project with Buddhist studies scholar Amy Langenberg that takes a survivor-centered approach to sexual abuse in Buddhism.[12] During the course of our research, we discovered that survivors of abuse in Buddhism and their allies find cult discourse very helpful as an interpretive lens and have adopted it as a way to identify, explain, and prevent abuse in Buddhist communities. I was also well aware that scholars of new religious movements (NRMs) and minority religions have staunchly opposed the term "cult," dismissed cult discourses, and undermined the credibility of abuse allegations by ex-members of these communities. Some of these scholars have also served as legal witnesses on behalf of groups accused of abuse and written passionately in their defense. Mayer became the target of rage because he was inaccurately perceived to be one such scholar. In this book, I want to examine this deep divide between survivors of abuse and scholars of NRMs/minority religions on the issue of abuse in "cults": an intensely emotional divide with profound ethical and legal as well as intellectual consequences. In my and Amy Langenberg's book, we trouble the ways in which Buddhist studies as a disciplinary field has failed to grapple with sexual abuse and misconduct in past and present forms of Buddhism.[13] Inspired by our collaborative interrogation of Buddhist studies, here I want to trouble the ways in which NRM scholars have, as Peljor appropriately put it, ignored the plight of survivors of abuse in minority religion. Over the course of these three chapters, I ask the following: Why have scholars of minority religion rejected the term "cult" and the wider field of cultic studies? How have they responded to allegations of abuse in minority religion? Why do so many survivors of abuse find cult discourse helpful? What new directions are emerging and should be encouraged in the study of NRMs that are more attuned to survivors' experiences?

In this chapter, I begin this investigation by considering the historic cultural context that led scholars to reject cult discourse and form a disciplinary consensus on abuse in NRMs and the ex-members who reported them. Then I discuss some critiques of this disciplinary consensus and the conditions in which it was formed, highlighting a largely ignored countercurrent of feminist scholars who have challenged the disciplinary consensus by calling attention to gendered and sexual violence in NRMs. Finally, inspired by this feminist lineage, I suggest a disciplinary reorientation toward evaluating the abuse allegations and the use of cult discourse among survivors of abuse.

ABUSE IN RELIGIOUS CONTEXTS

This book is concerned primarily with critiquing and offering a correction to the way consensus NRM scholarship has treated abuse allegations in NRMs. In our cowritten book, Amy Langenberg and I focus on sexual abuse in Buddhist communities. In this project, I interview survivors of sexual, psychological, and spiritual abuse, as well as victims of labor and other exploitation, in Buddhist communities. I adopt the definition of abuse in religious contexts from the Abuse in Religious Contexts research project, which was conducted in the United Kingdom between 2021 and 2024.[14] This explicitly survivor-centered project brought together a team of academic researchers and professionals with expertise in law to safe-guard and advocate for victim-survivors in order to understand abuse across a wide range of religious traditions and contexts. The project defines "abuse in religious contexts" as

> a person's experience of serious harm or exploitation caused by someone who has some form of religious power or control in relation to them. This power can be linked to an abuser's formal role in an organisation or the informal power that a person has through some form of religious status. It can involve power that comes from being seen as having particular inspiration or expertise (e.g. as a religious counsellor, healer, exorcist or teacher) or power that people have in a relationship because of shared religious assumptions.
>
> Such abuse can take a wide range of forms. The expressions and effects of abuse can be physical, sexual, emotional and psychological, financial and/or spiritual, and can include coercive control over a person's decisions and actions. Abuse can take the form both of a single, acute incident or of multiple experiences over a period of time.[15]

This broader definition of abuse and harm captures well the experience of the majority of my interviewees. While some were victims of sexual abuse and rape, others' experiences fell into the range of coercive control, spiritual abuse, and institutional betrayal.

NEW RELIGIOUS MOVEMENTS (NRMS), MINORITY RELIGIONS, AND CULTS

I use the designators "new religious movements" (NRMs) and "minority religions" interchangeably as the normative religious studies alternative terms to "cults." According to W. Michael Ashcraft, the origin of the term "NRM" is uncertain. One argument is that the term derived from a phrase that Japanese scholars used in the 1960s to describe emerging or previously suppressed religious groups.[16] Ashcraft adds that other terms have also emerged, such as "minority religions," "alternative religions," and "nontraditional religions," but that "NRM" remains the most popular term.[17] While NRM and other religious studies scholars have argued that the term "cult" is both meaningless and harmful, I use the term when referring directly to the perspectives and lived experiences of those who view certain religious groups as deserving of the term "cult" and unpack what exactly such interlocutors mean when they use the word "cult" or related designators such as "cultlike," "cultish," or "cultic dynamics." My approach here aligns with British sociologists Aled Thomas and Edward Graham-Hyde's recent suggestion that "it is important that scholarly research attempts to unpack the meanings intended by ex-members/leave-takers of minority religions when using 'cult' rhetoric. Furthermore, it is not the remit of scholars to make value judgements on the effective use of terminology when used by participants. Therefore, we argue that it is entirely justifiable to use the terminology when directly referring to the ideology of participants and those that have a lived reality that criticizes their previous religious identity/affiliation using 'cult' rhetoric."[18]

CULT DISCOURSE

In his 2018 book *A Historical Introduction to the Study of New Religious Movements*, W. Michael Ashcraft examines the field of cultic studies, which he identifies as the "intellectual wing of the anticult movement, whose members prefer the term cult critics."[19] Ashcraft notes that the main organizational home of cultic studies is the International Cultic Studies Association (ICSA), previously called the American Family Foundation (AFF).[20] He also offers a list of prominent names in cultic studies, including Michael Langone, Margaret Singer, Linda Dubrow-Marshall, Janja Lalich, and Daniel Shaw.[21] In his overview of cultic studies, Ashcraft focuses mainly on the trajectory of the theory of brainwashing, noting the influence of psychiatrists such as Robert Jay Lifton and Margaret Singer in its formation and promotion.[22] While Ashcraft offers a decent account of the main players and theories within the classic field of cultic studies, his history ends around 2013 and neglects many influential figures and new analytic developments.

Here I use the broader term "cult discourse" to include both classic cultic studies material and a wider range of resources that are being used to analyze and critique groups and dynamics. Cult discourse includes classic approaches such as those of Steven Hassan, whose Freedom of Mind Resource Center declares him to be "America's leading cult expert," and sociologist Janja Lalich, whose website describes her as "an international authority on cults, extremism, and coercion."[23] It also includes approaches like those of Alexandra Stein and Daniel Shaw, who draw heavily on psychoanalytic frameworks such as attachment theory and narcissism more than brainwashing theories to articulate relationships within cultic groups.[24]

The concept of spiritual abuse also plays a key role in cult discourse. While former ICSA executive director Michael Langone wrote about spiritual abuse as early as the mid-1990s, the concept has been developed and refined more recently.[25] Examining spiritual abuse in a Christian context, British researcher Lisa Oakley and activist Justin Humphreys define it as "a form of emotional and psychological abuse. It is characterized by a systematic pattern of coercive and controlling behavior in a religious context. Spiritual abuse can have a deeply damaging impact on those who experience it."[26]

Another major area of development in cult discourse is its overlap with feminist discourses on topics such as coercive control, gaslighting, grooming, and DARVO that connect survivors of "cults" and survivors of gendered violence and sexual abuse.[27] American sociologist Evan Stark developed the concept of coercive control to explain how male abusers developed power over their female victims in the context of domestic violence. He defined coercive control as a form of "entrapment" in which men "dominate individual women by interweaving repeated physical abuse with three equally important tactics: intimidation, isolation, and control."[28] Due to domestic violence advocacy work since the 1970s, coercive control became a criminal offense in family and intimate contexts in the United Kingdom in 2015.[29] Coercive control is defined as "an act or a pattern of acts of assault, threats, humiliation and intimidation or other abuse that is used to harm, punish, or frighten their victim."[30] Roderick P. Dubrow-Marshall developed the MSc Psychology of Coercive Control at the University of Salford, which seeks to examine "commonalities and differences in the forms of coercion and abusive practices across the domains of intimate partner violence, cults and extremist groups, trafficking gangs and organized crime."[31] Jennifer J. Freyd developed the concept of DARVO (Deny, Attack, and Reverse Victim and Offender) in 1997 to identify a common defense response among perpetrators of violence, particularly sexual violence, when confronted with their abusive behavior. Freyd extends DARVO from an individual to an institutional response with her concept of "institutional betrayal," which denotes how institutions fail to prevent or respond supportively to abuse and harm.[32]

In addition to analytic developments, multimedia has powered a new generation of cult discourse distribution. Often hosted by self-identified survivors of cults, influential podcasts include *IndoctriNation*, *A Little Bit Culty*, and *The Cult Vault*.[33] There has also been a proliferation of cult documentaries available on streaming platforms, such as *Holy Hell* (2016), *Wild Wild Country* (2018), and *Love Has Won* (2023). Another layer of cult discourse distribution involves figures who bridge different religious/spiritual subcultures and cultic studies. Writer and journalist Matthew Remski is one good example. He has published a number of influential pieces on abuse in yoga and Buddhist contexts and has used cult discourse as a main interpretive framework.[34] He is also the cohost of the podcast *Conspirituality*, which sets its goal as "dismantling New Age cults, wellness grifters, and conspiracy-mad yogis."[35]

These new developments—which denote both generational and analytic shifts within the anti-cult network, as well as ways in which cult discourse overlaps and has incorporated critiques originating outside of the anti-cult network—require much more diligent attention and careful contextualization than the default dismissal that marks the disciplinary consensus approach in NRM scholarship.[36]

"THE CULT WARS": THE CONTEXT FOR A NEW ACADEMIC SUBFIELD

The English term "cult" is derived from the Latin noun *cultus*, translated as religious worship or veneration. Its earliest recorded use is in the seventeenth century, when it was used to refer to any organized system of religious veneration.[37] According to Ashcraft, by the nineteenth century, the term was "commonly applied to any religious group that mainstream culture found objectionable (e.g. the Mormons, the Jehovah's Witnesses)."[38] American religious historian Sean McCloud highlights the function of cult rhetoric as a weapon of white middle class Christian hegemonic power through his examination of magazine coverage of "fringe religion" from the mid- to late twentieth century.[39] He shows that from 1959 to 1965, "cult" was used as a racist and classist derogatory term against religious groups composed of working-class white and Black Americans.[40]

While these examples show that the term "cult" had been operating in the mainstream as a negative term, sociologists of religion in the twentieth century were also using it as a neutral descriptive term to refer to a type of religious organization that was differentiated from a sect or a church.[41] Sociologists offered different typologies of cults, but the term generally signified a new religious group centered around a charismatic leader with unconventional beliefs and practices. Rodney Stark and William Sims Bainbridge, for instance, offered a threefold typology of cultic groups with each successive type—"audience cults," "client cults," and "cult movements"—denoting a higher level of commitment, organization, and religious compensation.[42]

During the 1970s, however, the term "cult" began to be solidified in mainstream culture as an essentialist pejorative term, leading to its replacement in scholarship by "new religious movement" (NRM) instead. The term's shift from a descriptive to a derogatory meaning was part of what is known as the "Cult Wars," a battle between NRMs and sociologists of religion on the one side and ex-members, parents of members, deprogrammers, psychologists, and journalists on the other. It was during the Cult Wars, whose beginnings are dated to the 1970s and 1980s, that the NRM consensus approach to abuse allegations was formed.

The Cult Wars themselves arose from broader culture wars. As historian Andrew Hartman notes, these culture wars began in the 1960s when the civil rights movement and the counterculture challenged the white middle-class normative culture of America. On one side was the "New Left," a loose configuration of movements that included the anti-war, Black Power, women's, and gay liberation movements, seeking racial, gender, and sexuality equality. On the other was a collation of conservative and Christian Right figures who believed the New Left was undermining the foundational Judeo-Christian values and beliefs of the nation.[43] Alongside and often interwoven with these radical sociocultural and political shifts was the emergence or rapid growth of a number of new religious communities. These included Christian-derived groups such as the Unification Church (1954) and the Children of God (1968), Hindu-derived groups such as the International Society for Krishna Consciousness (ISKCON, 1966), Buddhist groups such as Vajradhatu/Shambhala (1973), and entirely novel groups such as Scientology (1953).[44]

Scholars described this period as a time of great religious experimentation. Sociologist Robert Wuthnow declared that a "consciousness reformation" characterized the late 1960s, while religious studies scholar Jacob Needleman claimed that the "the turning of our young people to mysticism and Eastern religion is a phenomenon so various and pervasive" that "it was forming a 'new religious mind of young America.'"[45] McCloud, however, notes that "several scholars more historically removed from the period suggest that little statistical evidence supports the claim."[46] Nonetheless, the public perception of religious upheaval and the supposed emergence of unprecedented numbers of NRMs was threatening to many conservatives.

One early challenge to these groups came from conservative Christians who considered what they saw as cults to be a threat to the truth, authority, and membership numbers of Evangelical Christianity. These were part of the Christian Evangelical/Fundamentalist countercult lineage.[47] One example is Baptist pastor Walter Ralston Martin's 1965 book *The Kingdom of the Cults*, which defends "biblical Christianity" against what he claims is an avalanche of cults, with Jehovah's Witnesses, the Seventh-day Adventists, and the Mormons receiving particular attention.[48] Targeting cult leaders, Martin's book portrays cult members as lost souls in need of Christ's salvation. Evangelicals also started countercult organizations such as the Spiritual Counterfeits Project (SCP), which began in Berkeley, California, in the 1960s and later developed into a research institute that provides information about what it considers "false" or "counterfeit" religions.[49]

Further opposition to cults came from parents of children who were converting to new religious movements. The type of commitment demanded by these groups varied. But in many cases, young adult converts essentially renounced conventional society to live, work, and socialize fully in their new religious community, sometimes leaving college, jobs, and relationships to do so. Some parents of these adult converts believed that their children had been brainwashed by these groups and sought help from psychologists and deprogrammers. These concerned parties also began to form anti-cult organizations. In the summer of 1971, for instance, William Rambur, a retired navy officer from California, formed the Parents Committee to Free Our Sons and Daughters from the Children of God after his daughter, a twenty-two-year-old nursing student, joined the apocalyptic Evangelical group.[50]

Amplified by the media, concerned family members, psychologists, and deprogrammers began to promote a brainwashing narrative: namely, that these groups were led by fraudulent leaders who preyed on naïve and vulnerable young people and employed brainwashing techniques to recruit and keep them. To return these young adults to their real, "pre-brainwashed" selves, they argued, a deprogramming process was necessary.

As Ashcraft discusses, this brainwashing-deprogramming narrative arose against the historical backdrop of the Cold War and the Red Scare.[51] Americans saw communists as the antithesis of Americans: They were irrational masses who blindly followed their authoritarian leaders, in contrast to rational, freedom-loving, individualist Americans. During the Korean War (1950–3), thousands of American soldiers were taken prisoners by the Chinese and North Korean forces. When they were released, a very small number of these prisoners of war (POW) did not want to return to the United States, as they had become sympathetic to communism and critical of the United States, and the American public concluded that these

POWs had been brainwashed during their incarceration. Robert Jay Lifton, at the time a psychiatrist working in the U.S. Air Force, was one key figure in the formulation of this narrative. He interviewed a number of American soldiers and Chinese intellectuals who had been held in camps and published his findings in *Thought Reform and the Psychology of Totalism* (1961) in which he identifies eight psychological themes related to a culture of totalitarianism. Another influential figure was clinical psychologist Margaret Singer, who had also worked with American POWs returning from the Korean War. She conducted a study of 250 ex–cult members and drew similarities between them and American POWs. Singer would go on to appear as an expert witness in cases against cults/NRMs and to cowrite the classic cultic studies book *Cults in Our Midst: The Hidden Menace in our Everyday Lives* (1995).[52]

Convinced that their children had been brainwashed, parents began to pay deprogrammers to essentially abduct adult converts and subject them to a deprogramming process. As Ashcraft describes, "abductees would be kept against their will for days or weeks at a time. During this period of enforced isolation, deprogrammers, relatives and ex-members would engage the abductee, in an effort to persuade the targeted person to renounce the beliefs that he or she held as a member of an NRM . . . People supportive of deprogramming assumed that young adult converts had not joined NRMs willingly but had somehow been mentally manipulated to do so." Deprogrammers were not trained and varied in their methods. Perhaps the most notorious of these deprogrammers was Ted Patrick, author of the 1976 book *Let Our Children Go!*. During the 1970s, Patrick faced numerous criminal charges for false imprisonment and assault related to his deprogramming attempts. In 1976, he was convicted for one of these cases and sentenced to a year in prison.[53] Singer argued, however, that most deprogramming was much less controversial. In a 1978 article, she characterized it as consisting of "an intense period of information giving" by "reentry counselors," who had typically been members of cults themselves, followed by a period of healthy diet, sufficient sleep, and group therapy.[54]

Carol Giambalvo, Michael Kropveld, and Michael Langone give an account of this brainwashing-deprogramming period from the perspective of those involved in the North American Cult Awareness Movement (CAM). They claim that while parents were troubled that their children had dropped out of college to join these groups, their major concern was that their children displayed dramatic personality changes.[55] Parents also claimed that the groups had enforced separation between them and their children after they had made some progress in communicating their concerns. Giambalvo, Kropveld, and Langone add that "most mental health professionals . . . were uncomfortable with the sensationalized tone of much popular brainwashing literature" and were wary of deprogrammers.[56] They acknowledge, however, that the "nobody leaves a cult without deprogramming" myth dominated the lay discourse in the 1970s up to the late 1980s.[57]

In addition to individual deprogramming interventions, parents and anti-cult activists advocated for legal measures such as conservatorship laws and state intervention. The Peoples Temple tragedy in Jonestown in 1978, which saw the deaths of over nine hundred people—adults, children, and a U.S congressman—by murder or suicide, significantly bolstered public support for anti-cult activism. As CAM activists Giambalvo, Kropveld, and Langone state, "This tragedy caused the public to listen more closely to the CAM activists who had been speaking out about the broader problem of cults. Jonestown was an example of the worst possible outcome of cult activity. But within the CAM were people who could and did describe a range of personal tragedies, abuses, and pain that mesmerized the media."[58] In his examination of cult rhetoric in mainstream magazines, McCloud identifies the Jonestown tragedy as a major influence on negative journalistic coverage of new religious movements, with such groups now being seen as synonymous with authoritarianism, brainwashing, and coercion.[59] In the wake of Jonestown, a number of small secular organizations joined together in 1979 as the Citizens Freedom Foundation (CFF), which was renamed as the Cult Awareness Network (CAN) in 1984.[60] These activists called for state intervention and pushed for conservatorship legislation, which would enforce mental health evaluation of adult members.

It is within this very specific context of the popularity of the brainwashing-deprogramming narrative and legal battles against NRMs that scholarship on abuse in NRMs must be understood. The field of NRM scholarship formed essentially in reaction and as a corrective to the anti-cult movement. As Ashcraft puts it, "The American public's perception of New Religious Movements (NRMs) as fundamentally harmful cults stems from the 'anticult' movement of the 1970s which gave a somewhat hysterical and often distorted image of NRMs in the media. At the same time, academics pioneered a new field, studying these same NRMs from sociological and historical perspectives. They offered an interpretation that ran counter to that of the anticult movement. For these scholars in the field of NRM studies, NRMs were legitimate religions deserving of those freedoms granted to established religions."[61]

"THE CULT HOAX": THE FORMATION OF A DISCIPLINARY CONSENSUS

David G. Bromley and Anson D. Shupe's *Strange Gods: The Great American Cult Scare*, published in 1981, is a classic example of NRM scholars' response to the anti-cult movement and of the consensus approach to abuse allegations in NRMs.[62] Bromley and Shupe open by stating that no less than religious freedom and civil liberties are at stake in the study of NRMs. They identify two forces against NRMs: a coalition of groups known as the anti-cult movement, composed of family members of young adults who have converted to NRMs as well as deprogrammers, and a set of fundamentalist Christian organizations that attack NRMs on theological grounds. They also point to media reports that depict an "overblown cultural hysteria" about the number of people caught up in cults and the circulation of "horror stories" from "disillusioned or disgruntled ex-members" who "have been able to sway audiences and actually incite mobs with their inflammatory accusations and lurid claims."[63]

As a counter to these media reports, Bromley and Shupe make two primary moves. The first is to locate such allegations in a historic lineage of false and lurid allegations made against minority religions. For instance, they give examples of nineteenth-century Protestant anti-Catholic propaganda that depicted Catholic priests as sexually deprived. The second is to examine accusations made against six specific NRMs: the Children of God, the Unification Church, ISKCON, the Divine Light Mission, Scientology, and the Peoples Temple. They argue that only the Peoples Temple was a site of real violence and that the other groups have been unfairly targeted by "angry ex-members" who have fabricated "stories of atrocities that include lurid themes of exploitation, manipulation, and deception," in order to justify coercive actions against NRMs.[64] Similarly, they report that anti-cultist family members have "flooded the media with tales of brainwashing and enslavement."[65] Bromley and Shupe conclude that "the new religions have more often been the victims than the perpetrators of violence" and argue that it is essential to defend them and protect religious freedom.[66]

Strange Gods set the ground for what became the consensus view among sociologists of religion on NRMs:

1. "Cult" is a biased, subjective and stigmatizing term.[67]
2. Abuse allegations in NRMs are simply "atrocity tales" and should be discredited.
3. Ex-members, or "apostates," are manipulative and unreliable.
4. NRMs are more the victims than the perpetrators of violence.
5. The anti-cult movement is a vehicle of normative Christian or state power and a threat to religious freedom.
6. Scholars should defend NRMs on both an intellectual and legal level.[68]

While all of these assumptions have shaped NRM scholars' approach to abuse allegations, two are particularly significant: the atrocity tale and the stance on apostates or ex-members.[69]

ATROCITY TALES AND APOSTATES

One of the earliest articulations of the atrocity tale model came in David G. Bromley, Anson D. Shupe, and J. C. Ventimiglia's 1979 article "Atrocity Tales, the Unification Church, and the Social Construction of Evil."[70] They argue anti-cult activists made atrocity allegations against the Unification Church to evoke public outrage in order to assert normative social control over it. In other words, what these scholars call the "atrocity tale" is a weapon used to achieve dominance over religious minorities. As they describe it, "An *atrocity* may be defined as an event which is viewed as a flagrant violation of a fundamental cultural value. Accordingly, an *atrocity tale* is a presentation of that event (real or imaginary) in such a way as to a) evoke moral outrage by specifying and detailing the value violations, b) authorize, implicitly or explicitly, punitive sanctions, and c) mobilize control efforts against the alleged perpetrators." Strikingly, the authors not only separate the question of the *truth* of the atrocity tale from the *function* of the atrocity tale but go as far to say that the former is irrelevant. They continue, "It is not of importance whether the allegations made in atrocity stories are actually true or false. . . . Whether such stories represent some kernel of 'truth' is not only difficult to validate in many cases but is also irrelevant. The stories gain their persuasiveness and motivating power from their larger-than-life quality."[71] Using a sample of 190 articles written by former members of the Unification Church and published between 1974 and 1977, they conclude that each accusation has been embellished and signals either a legal misdemeanor, a violation of conventional society, or an instance of racialization.[72] They identify the most potent weapon against the marginalized group as the ex-member or "apostate." As they continue, "The apostate plays a significant role in discrediting a deviant group and in authorizing social control measures. He or she can reveal the group's inner workings and secrets in such a way as to confirm suspicions and allegations about it, condemn the group with a knowledge and certainty no outsider could muster, and reaffirm the values of conventional society by voluntarily and publicly confessing the 'error' of his or her ways."[73]

Written over forty years ago, Bromley, Shupe, and Ventimiglia's critical portrayal of ex-members and the atrocity tale became the dominant narrative within religious studies scholarship. In 1994, British sociologist Bryan R. Wilson, for instance, wrote a foundational article that discredited ex-members. In his words,

> Neither the objective sociological researcher nor the court of law can readily regard the apostate as a creditable or reliable source of evidence. He must always be seen as one whose personal history predisposes him to bias with respect to both his previous religious commitment and affiliations, [and] the suspicion must arise that he acts from a personal

> motivation to vindicate himself and to regain his self-esteem, by showing himself to have been first a victim but subsequently to have become a redeemed crusader. As various instances have indicated, he is likely to be suggestible and ready to enlarge or embellish his grievances to satisfy that species of journalist whose interest is more in sensational copy than in an objective statement of the truth."[74]

Notably, Wilson's undermining of ex-member testimony is reproduced on the Scientology website as well as the website of Scientologists Taking Action Against Discrimination, where it undoubtedly functions as a legitimation source for their religion.[75] In a more recent 2024 publication, George D. Chryssides reiterates the consensus view on ex-members. He states, "Much recent anticult rhetoric, including brainwashing theory, comes from ex-members. Ex-member testimony has to be regarded with some caution, and NRM scholars have characteristically been wary of it, not to say dismissive. It should be kept in mind, as Stephen E. Gregg and I have pointed out, that it is only the vociferous members that tend to get heard. They are the ones that no doubt had bad experiences, have become embittered, and want to warn others or harbour grudges which they want to avenge by recounting atrocity tales." Chryssides continues that there are many reasons that people leave NRMs that do not involve "grievance," but it is those he labels as "vociferous leavers, who join ex-member groups or anti-cult organizations" that are more accessible to the researcher.[76]

Phillip C. Lucas notes that scholars of NRMs often employ a triangulation method when researching groups. Triangulation is a social science methodology that involves gathering information from multiple sources to gain as objective a view as possible. As Lucas explains, scholars interview current members, ex-members, and people in the wider community who have contact with, or knowledge of, the NRM in question and cross-check these sources with external written sources such as media coverage and other forms of documentation in order to construct the most accurate portrayal of the group.[77] While this triangulation method is a scholarly ideal, the reality is that not only has the "unreliable apostate" narrative significantly undermined the credibility of ex-members for researchers, but ex-members themselves often view NRM scholars with suspicion as a result. In addition, groups such as Scientology have refused to work with researchers whose work they cannot vet and researchers who work with ex-members.[78]

WHAT THE CONSENSUS VIEW GETS RIGHT

Scholars representing the consensus view have made a number of invaluable intellectual and ethical contributions to the study of NRMs. These contributions have been discussed extensively elsewhere and form the mainstream of scholarly approaches to NRMs, so I only briefly name them here. Analytically, it is true that the term "cult" is a subjective, imprecise, and biased term. It is almost impossible to objectively distinguish between legitimate religion and illegitimate cults.[79] American religious historians such as Sean McCloud and Richard Kent Evans have also highlighted how classism and racism can determine which religious groups are defined as cults.[80] Though cult deprogramming methods were varied, some did involve kidnapping and physical and psychological violence, and some resulted in criminal convictions.[81]

The "cult" label has been directly weaponized by dominant religious and political groups to target socially vulnerable minority religions, with anti-cult discourse reaching an apex during the Satanic Panic of the 1980s.[82] The term "cult" has also circulated in the media in sensationalist and dehumanizing ways. This has resulted in stigmatization, harm, and violence. NRM scholar Catherine Wessinger argues that the naming of the group as a cult by the media "creates a climate in which the public accepts what might actually be excessive action or force against these communities."[83] One of the most devastating examples of this is the Waco siege, which saw the deaths of seventy-six men, women, and children in a fire after FBI agents launched a gas attack on the Branch Davidian compound in Waco, Texas. Wessinger suggests that "the application of the term 'cult' to the Branch Davidians helped create a social context in which FBI agents could wage psychological warfare against the community and carry out the tank and gas assault that culminated in the devastating fire."[84] She points to a 1993 CNN/Gallup poll that found that 73 percent of Americans thought the decision to gas the Branch Davidians was a "responsible" one.

WHAT THE CONSENSUS VIEW GETS WRONG

While scholars of NRM have done an excellent job at identifying harm perpetuated *against* minority religions, they have fallen significantly short in identifying abuse that occurs *by and within* them. Since the 1960s, a number of NRMs have faced allegations of sexual, physical, and psychological abuse as well as financial and labor exploitation. Recent years have witnessed many of these allegations being substantiated and publicly acknowledged. One example is 3HO, the Healthy, Happy, Holy Organization founded in 1969 in the United States by the Indian spiritual leader and entrepreneur Yogi Bhajan (1929–2004). In 2020, Pamela Saharah Dyson, who had been the personal secretary of Yogi Bhajan, published a memoir that alleged that for decades he had been abusive and coerced her and other female students into sex with him.[85] Other women also came forward with allegations of sexual abuse after Dyson's book was published. Following this, the Siri Singh Sahib

Corporation (SSSC), an entity that includes 3HO, commissioned an independent investigation that found that Yogi Bhajan had "more likely than not" committed a wide range of abuses against women and female minors that included rape, sexual battery, sexual abuse, sexual harassment, physical abuse, and other forms of coercive behavior.[86] Within the year, multiple adult survivors of sexual, psychological, spiritual, and physical abuse in 3HO boarding schools also came forward. In 2025, SSSC published the results of an "Independent Healing and Reparations Program for the 3HO/Sikh Dharma Community," which acknowledged that "harmful experiences have occurred along with all the positive, transformational and life-changing experiences within the community."[87] Reporting on the case, journalist Stacie Stukin and American religious historian Philip Deslippe succinctly note, "nearly 600 survivors filed claims alleging thousands of incidents of abuse."[88]

Another example is the Jesus Fellowship Church, a U.K. Evangelical Christian group that was founded by charismatic preacher Noel Stanton (1926–2009) in 1969. In 2015, the local county police launched Operation Lifeboat to investigate over 130 complaints of abuse in the group ranging from emotional abuse to serial sexual abuse. It resulted in five criminal convictions, four of which involved abuse against minors. In 2018, ten former members began the Jesus Fellowship Survivors Association, which, following legal advice, focused on a redress scheme to enable victims to seek compensation rather than pursue legal charges. As the British broadsheet *The Guardian* reported, "The redress scheme's final report, published in September 2024, was staggering. It found that there were 264 alleged abusers within the fellowship, of whom more than half were leaders. One in six children who lived in [church-owned housing] was estimated to have been abused between 1969 and 2019. Over 30 allegations related to Stanton himself. The trustees wrote: 'Harm and abuse were not limited to a handful of leaders, a particular period of time, or geographical locations. It was widespread and systematic.'"[89]

Notably, awareness of abuse in these cases was brought about by survivors and ex-members of the groups speaking out and advocating for justice, and their efforts have been covered by mainstream media in newspapers and documentaries. It is also notable that there have been no focused treatments, and little acknowledgment, of such abuse in NRM consensus scholarship.[90] Moreover, NRM consensus scholars have defended many groups accused of—and in some cases, legally found to have committed—such abuse. In *Strange Gods: The Great American Cult Scare*, for instance, Bromley and Shupe declared ISKCON to be harmless. Just seven years later, in 1988, members of the group and sociologist E. Burke Rochford Jr. publicly acknowledged extensive child abuse and institutional cover-up.[91] In 2005, ISKCON paid a total of $9.5 million to approximately 450 alleged victims of sexual, physical, and emotional abuse that took place in the 1970s and 1980s at its boarding schools in the United States and India.[92] One of the most dramatic failures of NRM consensus scholars was the case of Aum Shinrikyo, a Japanese minority religious group, which was suspected of a sarin gas attack on the Tokyo subway system that killed twelve people in 1995. Aum Shinrikyo had already been accused of many serious crimes, including torture, kidnapping and murder. Shortly after the sarin attack, James R. Lewis and J. Gordon Melton travelled to Japan to defend the group. Despite having no research history with Aum Shinrikyo and not speaking Japanese, Lewis assumed and protested their innocence and called on the police to uphold their religious freedom in a press conference. Aum Shinrikyo members themselves, however, soon after admitted to carrying out the murders.[93]

In his 2018 *A Historical Introduction to the Study of New Reli-*

gious Movements, Ashcraft acknowledges the failure of NRM scholars to address forms of violence other than suicide and homicide in NRMs. As Ashcraft explains, "Violent acts and intentions fall on a spectrum, according to many variables, like individual vs. collective, or criminal vs. non-criminal. The momentum of NRM-related scholarship thus far has neglected violence that falls short of being deadly."[94] He argues that NRM studies needs a broader definition of violence and acknowledges that NRM scholars would benefit from drawing from the more comprehensive analyses of abuse developed by cultic studies.[95]

While Ashcraft avoids tackling the issue of why NRM scholars have ignored abuse in NRMs, other critics have tied their failure to a commitment to defending NRMs against the anti-cult movement and their prioritization of religious freedom over all other concerns. These critics have argued, persuasively in my view, that such a commitment has led to both intellectual and ethical failures: namely, poor scholarship and a minimization of abuse in NRMs. In their pointedly titled 1998 article "Academic Compromise in the Social Scientific Study of Alternative Religions," sociologist Stephen A. Kent and Theresa Krebs argued that objective analysis is compromised when academics become intentionally involved in, or are inadvertently co-opted by, religious organizations in their efforts to gain legitimacy.[96] Tracing such collaboration back to NRM scholars' involvement with the Unification Church, they discuss two case studies in which NRM movements recruited scholars when faced with legal allegations of abuse and negative media and public perceptions.[97]

Kent and Krebs note, for example, that one unnamed group faced a court case in the United Kingdom involving the sexual abuse of children. The founder of this group had doctrinally encouraged sexual activity between adults and children, and the group had been subject to many accusations of sexual abuse of children. In order to counter negative press, the group reached out to NRM scholars, who produced an edited volume with chapters based on researchers' visits to group homes. This study was then used as public relations material by the group.[98] However, as Kent and Krebs record, "the organization specifically designed what it internally called 'media homes,' which are the very sites that researchers visited. Handpicked individuals living in these well-funded facilities went through rehearsals about how to portray themselves and the group to media, scholars, and others who might scrutinize them. Subsequently, former members have reported how these media homes operated, even describing the drills and rehearsals in which they participated."[99]

Krebs and Kent also give examples of NRM scholars serving as expert witnesses in court, defending groups against allegations made by former members. In a case brought against the Church of Scientology, for instance, an NRM scholar provided support for the Church of Scientology to keep its upper-level documents secret on the grounds that secrecy is a core practice of many religions. While this is historically true, Kent and Krebs point out that "academics should realize that religious organizations frequently use secrets to cover instances of manipulation and abuse."[100]

In a blistering 2001 critique of the Aum Shinrikyo episode, psychology professor Benjamin Beit-Hallahmi argues that, rather than the exception, scholars' misguided advocacy on behalf NRMs is the "party line" within academia.[101] As Beit-Hallahmi explains, Lewis and Melton "were acting out of a certain mind-set, which to them was not just reasonable but commendable. The Aum episode was symptomatic of an ideology that sees our world as a place in which NRMs are maliciously attacked by forces of the state and are always presumed to be innocent."[102] Beit-Hallahmi continues by interrogating the "hierarchy of credibility" in which self-presentation by NRMs (the insider perspective) is considered epistemologically superior to outside accounts (such as those by ex-members) and that he sees as reaching a "logical conclusion" in the Aum Shinrikyo case. He identifies an "ideology of collaborationism" in which scholars act as legitimation agents for NRM movements and traces its origin to a 1989 memo between senior NRM scholars that shows a coordinated plan to work with NRM groups to counter the anti-cult movement.[103] Beit-Hallahmi concludes that such collaborationism has resulted in the minimization and ignoring of any harmful behavior that threatens the legitimacy of minority religion and the replacement of critical scholarship by apologetics and propaganda.[104]

"WE WERE NOT SILENT BUT ACTUALLY SILENCED": THE FEMINIST LINEAGE

Critics of NRM consensus scholars argue that the latter's choice to ignore abuse in NRMs came as a result of their attempt to counter cultic studies scholars' exaggeration of abuse. There were other, non–cultic studies scholars, however, who were also raising concerns about abuse in NRMs and about the silence of NRM consensus scholars about such abuse.[105] In Mary Jo Neitz and Marion S. Goldman's 1995 edited collection *Sex, Lies, and Sanctity: Religion and Deviance in North America*, a few contributors attempt to counter such silence by offering structural analyses of abuse in religious contexts. Robert W. Balch, for instance, opens his chapter by noting that despite increasing exposés of abuse in NRMs, sociologists have ignored abuse because of their objections to the anti-cult movement. He writes, "Unfortunately, we lack systemic evidence about the extent of corruption or its causes because sociologists have ignored the issue. Anti-cult writers have tried to call attention to corruption in new religions for years, but social scientists have dismissed their claims on the grounds that the charges are based on sensationalism, bad evidence and ethnocentrism."[106] Drawing on his own ethnographic work with the Love Family, a communal religion group formed in 1968, Balch identified a number of structural factors that enabled abusive behavior. These included unquestioning obedience to charismatic authority, which resulted in leaders being granted exceptions from the rules that governed others, and a system of information control and secrecy. Balch credits ex-members, or "cult defectors," with playing a key role in blowing the whistle on abuse in these groups. Extending these findings beyond his own research population, Balch concludes that "there are enough structural similarities between the Love Family and other charismatic cults to suggest that corruption probably is more common in new religions than social scientists realize. He emphasizes that, in groups like these, "no evidence doesn't mean no abuse" as "members are very good at information control."[107]

It is notable these chapters appeared in an edited collection by Neitz and Goldman, sociologists who specialized in gender, as it was feminist scholars of religion who were at the forefront of identifying abuse in NRMs. They raised concerns about patriarchal misogynist groups and offered structural critiques of abuse within NRMs. Some of these frameworks share points of analytic similarity with cult critical models, but these feminist scholars were not aligned with the anti-cult movement and rarely used cult rhetoric. As early as 1978, feminist theologian Emily Culpepper made the case that NRMs only offered a "pseudo-newness for women," as behind superficial differences, the roles for women remained "heavily traditional, patriarchal ones," which were often reinforced by misogynist theologies.[108] Culpepper also critiqued the "more individualistic" groups—such as Zen and yoga—which only offered women a sense of peace within a "largely unchallenged patriarchal status quo."[109] She concluded, "Many cults offer only yet another male guru/deity/leader whose insights and directions women are again supposed to trust and follow."[110]

Perhaps the most sustained critique of gendered abuse in NRMs has been developed by sociologist Janet Liebman Jacobs.[111] In her 1989 book *Divine Disenchantment: Deconverting from New Religions*, Jacobs points out that NRM scholars had focused their research on ex-members on those who were deprogrammed or forced to exit NRMs. As a counter, she interviews forty people who left NRMs on their own accord.[112] She finds that abusive teacher behavior, including sexual violence, and an emerging feminist consciousness around the patriarchal structures of these groups were major factors in these ex-members' deconversion processes.[113] Drawing on sociology, psychoanalysis, and feminist theory, Jacobs argues that for many members, NRMs function as an idealized substitute family, and the gendered violence that occurs within these groups often parallels that of the nuclear family, such as incest and domestic violence.

In a chapter in the 2000 edited collection *Bad Pastors: Clergy Misconduct in Modern America*, Jacobs provides an incisive structural critique of patriarchal charismatic groups.[114] Drawing on ex-member testimony from a range of NRM groups including Buddhist ones, Jacobs shows how male entitlement to sex with women and children is a core feature of these groups. Without explicitly referencing cult discourse, Jacobs identifies many of the same characteristics that cult critical frameworks also flag, such as an authoritarian male teacher, a hierarchical group structure, an elite inner circle, the enforcement of sanctions, and group insularity. Rather than "othering" these groups, however, Jacobs stresses continuity between abuse in NRMs and society at large, arguing that such groups are microcosms of the society they are situated in. In her words, "As charismatic leaders assume the role of patriarchal authority within religious communities, their abuse of power can be situated within the discourse on the commodification and sexual objectification of women in patriarchal society."[115]

Jacobs has also levelled a powerful critique at the refusal of NRM scholars to tackle abuse in NRMs. In her 2007 chapter "Abuse in New Religious Movements: Challenges for the Sociology of Religion," Jacobs argues that NRM scholars have narrowly defined what counts as violence—focusing solely on extreme acts of murder and mass suicide—and have trivialized other forms of physical or sexual violation. Their lack of understanding of gender-based violence, she contends, has had particularly harmful consequences for women and children in NRM groups.[116] While feminist researchers had identified violence and abuse in NRMs as early as the 1980s, she argues that their scholarship was largely ignored in the wider field. In her words:

> For the most part, the sociological literature on NRMs has avoided the difficult questions of gendered violence and sexual exploitation, emphasizing instead the constructive and functional aspects of religious commitment. In an effort to protect religious freedom and to counter the stigma typically associated with alternative religious groups, scholars in the sociology of religion have often been reluctant to recognize and discuss the abusive practices of these movements, despite the violence identified in the research. At academic conferences and in reviews of the literature, feminist scholars who have brought these abuses to the attention of their colleagues have been heavily critiqued and the accounts of their informants have come under attack and are viewed with suspicion.[117]

Sociologist Mary Jo Neitz also notes the barriers feminists have faced when trying to name abuse in religions. She explains, "In a context where sociologists were defending marginal religion against popular attacks, it was initially difficult to get a hearing for sociological work that was actually critical of sects and cults. When feminist researchers began to uncover stories of sexual abuse of female devotees by leaders, for example, they had to figure out how to frame their critical concerns in ways that would not exacerbate generalized biases against cults and sects."[118] In a personal conversation, sociologist Marion S. Goldman further explained that it was not just a case of feminist scholars having to work out how to best articulate concerns in a hostile climate; they also faced significant opposition in the field of NRM scholarship in general. She pointedly stated, "Much of our work was rejected by the *JSSR* [*Journal of the Scientific Study of Religion*] and other journals because of our feminism. We were not silent but actually silenced."[119]

FROM ATROCITY TALE TO SURVIVOR-CENTERED: REORIENTING APPROACHES TO ABUSE

Scholars of minority religion have offered invaluable critiques of the ways that the term "cult" can and has been employed to cause harm against marginalized groups. Yet as both critics of the consensus approach in NRM scholarship and feminist scholars of NRMs have amply demonstrated, this has come at a significant cost to victim-survivors of abuse within these groups. Following the feminist lineage, and inspired by Jacobs's significant interventions in particular, I argue that there needs to be a significant reorientation in NRM scholarship toward ex-members or those who have suffered abuse in minority religious groups. I suggest that a more ethical orientation is a survivor-centered approach. Survivor-centered approaches "actively center the perspectives and needs of survivors of sexual violence. As a feminist approach, this reframing critically addresses and dismantles the hierarchies of knowledge and truth that tend to structure how we think about and research sexual violence."[120] In our research process for our upcoming book on sexual abuse in contemporary Buddhist contexts, Amy Langenberg and I became aware of how normative disciplinary formation within Buddhist studies unintentionally decentered and erased the experiences of survivors of abuse. We chose to take a survivor-centered approach to abuse because we had to actively push against the grain of normative Buddhist studies approaches in order to make survivors' voices audible.[121] We argue that without a survivor-centered approach, scholarship risks merely reproducing "normative Buddhist constellations of power—the same dynamics that tolerate and engender abuse."[122]

We were inspired to adopt a survivor-centered approach by intersectional feminist Sara Ahmed's work on formal complaints of sexual and racial discrimination and violence in university settings.[123] Ahmed suggests that we can only fully learn how institutional systems of power operate by listening to those who power operates *on*—in other words, those located outside power and those whom power routinely silences. For Ahmed, this type of listening is the mark of a feminist sensibility. In her words, "To hear with a feminist ear is to hear who is not heard. . . . If we are taught to tune out some people, then a feminist ear is an achievement. We become attuned to those who are tuned out."[124] In our research project, Langenberg and I had to learn how to listen to survivors of abuse, a process that "opened up new epistemological horizons and ethical commitments for our collaborative, co-authored book project."[125]

One way to start to listen to those who have been "tuned out" of the field of NRM scholarship—namely, ex-members or those who have suffered abuse in minority religious groups—is to acknowledge and become curious about the language they use to articulate their experiences. Listening to survivors necessitates that NRM scholars reorient their approach to cult discourse. Rather than automatically dismiss it, I suggest that scholars begin to ask questions about its meaning, function, and value for survivors. Such questions include the following: What type of cult discourse do survivors use? What functions does cult discourse serve for survivors? In what ways do survivors find cult discourse helpful? In what ways do they find it unhelpful? What other discourses do survivors draw on alongside cult discourse? In the next chapter, I explore the results of this survivor-centered approach to cult discourse in interviews I undertook with a group of survivors of abuse in contemporary Buddhist contexts.

CHAPTER 2

"We Can't Fix Something If We Can't Name It"

The Function of Cult Discourse for Survivors

Visibly relaxed as she chatted with me over Zoom, Nancy Floy, cofounder of a support group for survivors of abuse in Buddhist contexts, enthusiastically affirmed the usefulness of cult discourse for survivors. As she explained, "I think the cult model is excellent. The majority of the survivors who I am working with—and now it is a lot because of our program—relate to the cult model and find it helpful." Drawing from her own history in successive Tibetan Buddhist communities, Floy explained that many cult dynamics—which she named as "grooming," "indoctrination," "complete deference to the leader," and "deception"—became evident once she joined the groups' inner circles. I asked how she had come to learn about cult dynamics. She paused and responded, "When I got out of Shambhala, I was just desperate for some understanding of what happened. I got out . . . and there wasn't that much written [about abuse in Buddhism] at that time. . . . But the cult material, you know, that was what was there, that was what was there to help."[1]

Nancy is one of the cofounders of Heartwood's Connecting Survivors of Teacher and Guru Abuse program, a group that she began with Rachel Montgomery in 2021 to support survivors of abuse in Buddhist contexts.[2] The group, whose members are spread across the United States and Europe, meets virtually once a month.

Heartwood also hosts a women-only small group that is facilitated by Rachel Bernstein, a marriage and family therapist with a specialization in cult recovery and the host of popular cult-critical podcast *IndoctriNation*.[3]

In this chapter, I draw on interviews with thirteen members of the Heartwood survivors' group to unpack the multiple ways that they use cult discourse and to highlight the specific functions it serves for them. In conclusion, I consider what these survivor voices can add to scholarship on abuse and cult discourse in NRMs and minority religions. First, however, some context on my research populations, methodology, and position is necessary.

RESEARCH POPULATIONS: CONVERT BUDDHISTS

My interviewees are self-identified survivors of abuse—sexual, psychological, and spiritual—in what scholars have referred to as "convert Buddhist" communities. While Buddhism is a world religion, it is a minority religion in the United States. A 2025 Pew study, for example. found that just 1 percent of adults identify as Buddhists in North America.[4]

Buddhism was first brought to the United States by Chinese and Japanese immigrants in the mid-nineteenth century. These communities built the first Buddhist temples, established the first Buddhist organizations, and preserved Buddhist practice in the face of intense racial violence, religious discrimination, and legal exclusions.[5] During the 1960s and 1970s, Asian Buddhists and white North Americans who had trained with Buddhist monastic and lay teachers in Asia established convert Buddhist centers and organizations that catered to mostly white American and European students.

Scholars described these emerging lineages as "convert" Buddhists to distinguish them from "immigrant" or "heritage" Asian American Buddhist communities.[6] Drawing from the Theravāda, Zen, and Tibetan traditions, these communities were historically composed of white, upper-middle-class practitioners and primarily focused on meditation practice.[7] These convert groups were often referred to in the media and academic scholarship as new religious movements. This was particularly true of groups begun by and centered around charismatic Asian teachers, such as the Vajradhatu/Shambhala community, founded by the Tibetan Buddhist teacher Chögyam Trungpa (1939–87).

Since the 1980s, many of these Buddhist convert communities have been rocked by sexual abuse and misconduct allegations and cases.[8] These have cut across Buddhist lineages and racial and ethnic lines and included first, second, and even third generations of teachers. An early case involved Richard Baker, the dharma heir of Shunryū Suzuki (1904–71), who founded the San Francisco Zen Center (SFZC). The married Baker was forced to resign as abbot of the SFZC in 1984 after having multiple affairs with female students and facing complaints of financial impropriety.[9] In December 1988, it was revealed that Ösel Tendzin (1943–90), Trungpa's American successor, had been having unprotected sex with his students despite knowing he was HIV positive. Tendzin and a male student he slept with later died of AIDS-related causes. The student's girlfriend also contracted the disease but survived.[10] In November 1994, a former student known only as Janice Doe filed a lawsuit against popular Tibetan teacher Sogyal Rinpoche (1947–2019) and Rigpa, the transnational Buddhist organization he founded, alleging "fraud, assault and battery, infliction of emotional distress, and breach of fiduciary duty."[11]

In 2010, journalist Mark Oppenheimer published a story titled

"Sex Scandal Has U.S. Buddhists Looking Within," which detailed four decades' worth of sexual harassment and misconduct allegations against Rinzai Zen teacher Eido Shimano (1932–2018), who founded the first Zen monastery in the United States.[12] Similarly, Rinzai teacher Joshu Sasaki (1907–2014) allegedly engaged in sexual abuse and harassing behavior for decades before being publicly accused for the first time in a student's blog post in 2012.[13]

The MeToo movement reignited a conversation about sexual harm in Buddhist communities. In 2017, Sogyal Rinpoche was forced to resign after a letter written by eight senior Rigpa students, including a nun and a former director, alleging decades of extreme physical, sexual, psychological, and emotional violence perpetrated by him, went viral.[14] He had denied allegations of sexual violence for decades and been fully supported by Rigpa leaders. The public release of this letter, however, finally forced him to resign as spiritual director and compelled Rigpa to employ a third-party safeguarding investigation.[15] In 2018, *The New York Times* ran a story titled "The 'King' of Shambhala Buddhism Is Undone by Abuse Report," which revealed that Sakyong Mipham Rinpoche, Trungpa's son and the leader of Shambhala, had stepped down from his position after facing multiple allegations of sexual misconduct brought about by the survivor-centered Buddhist initiative Project Sunshine.[16] Accounts of these cases and many other cases of alleged abuse in Buddhist contexts are included on the International Cultic Studies Association (ICSA) website, under the title "Buddhist Aberrations."[17]

RESEARCH METHOD AND POSITION

I interviewed thirteen participants from the Heartwood Connecting Survivors of Guru and Teacher Abuse program using semistructured interview questions.[18] Most participants regularly attended the Heartwood group; a couple had only attended a few sessions but remained subscribed to the group's email list. Twelve participants were white women ranging from their early thirties to late sixties. One was a man in his thirties who identified as mixed-race.[19] All identified as survivors of abuse in Buddhist contexts, with a range of specific experiences including sexual, psychological, and spiritual abuse as well as boundary violations, labor exploitation, and institutional betrayal. Most of my interlocutors had practiced in convert Buddhist communities for decades; several had lived in Buddhist communities; others were relatively new practitioners when they experienced abuse. Some participants still identified as Buddhists, while others had left the tradition. Only one remained in the community that they had experienced abuse in because the teacher responsible for the abuse had been removed. While there was a wide variety in participants' levels of engagement with cult discourse, all were interested in participating in the study because they felt that cult discourse had played some role in their recovery process. My interviews with them lasted from one to three hours, with follow up correspondence in some cases.

It is important to acknowledge my distinct research position. I became connected to the Heartwood group through my collaborative survivor-centered research on sexual abuse in Buddhism with Amy Langenberg.[20] During that research, we interviewed several members of the Heartwood group, became Advisory Board members, and co-organized a conference with Heartwood and Northwestern University on sexual violence in Buddhism, with a focus on survivors' voices, in October 2024.[21] I had interviewed six out of the thirteen interviewees before and met three others at the conference. As such, they knew me as an academic advocate for survivors of abuse in Buddhist contexts, which undoubtedly impacted both their willingness to be interviewed and the interview content.

My methodological approach is rooted in the postcolonial feminist lineage of anthropology, which advances ethnography as an act of identification and witnessing. An early expression of this is Ruth Behar's articulation of a "native anthropology," in which scholars claim a personal connection to their ethnographic sites and view identity rather than difference as key to research.[22] Nancy Scheper-Hughes extends this with her "anthropology of witnessing," in which fieldwork is intentionally undertaken as an act of empathy and protest.[23] My methodology is a deliberate intervention within and counter to the NRM consensus approach, in which survivors of abuse who use cult discourse have been largely ignored and/or undermined as credible epistemological sources.

RESEARCH FINDINGS

In addition to discovering the different ways that Heartwood members define a cult, and the type of cult discourse they were engaging in and the depth of that engagement, I identified six functions that cult discourse served for them:

1. Naming
2. Healing
3. Warning and prevention
4. Community
5. Slippage between religious experience and traumatic experience
6. Gender critique

In addition to naming the specific ways they found cult discourse helpful, Heartwood members also pointed out limits and critiques of cult discourse. I unpack each theme below.

DEFINITIONS

"Cult is something I am not in," stated Tess when prompted to define a cult. "Cult is perhaps in a desert in America, completely cut off. They maybe have multiple wives. They have very strange beliefs."[24] In contrast, she noted how one of the first things she saw when she walked into her urban Buddhist center was a set of photographs of famous politically progressive people with the teachers. These photographs, highlighting the relationship between Buddhism and human rights discourse, signaled authenticity and safety to her. For Tess, a European woman in her thirties, her stereotype of a cult had prevented her seeing what she later came to identify as "the cultic dynamics" in her community. Several of my interlocutors acknowledged that cult was difficult to define and was a "harsh," "loaded," and "limited" term that "stereotyped" and "pigeonholed" people and groups. As Rachel reflected, "I don't find there's a way to find a term that's all encompassing [like cult] without stereotyping."[25] Nonetheless, several core characteristics were echoed across interviews: a controlling teacher, a hierarchical group structure, a culture of insiders and outsiders, the use or misuse of spiritual teachings to exert control, a complicit and deferential community, an erasure of individual conscience, and the threat or actuality of expulsion if one dissented. Betty, a European woman in her late sixties, had suffered physical, psychological, and sexual abuse in successive yoga and Buddhist communities. She had attempted suicide and credited Heartwood for "saving her life." For Betty, the concentrated power of the teacher was paramount. As she explained, "There is really only one person in charge. . . . Even when they have committees and all that stuff, whatever that head person says, everybody will do. . . . And when you're fighting it, you become an outcast."[26] Wongmo, who had left her community because of its cover-up of teacher sexual abuse, emphasized the way that cults encourage the sacrifice of individual integrity for group conformity. In her words, "I think of a social grouping where there is intense pressure to share a worldview and conduct, accompanied by an erosion of trust in one's own individual sources of wisdom and power."[27]

Darren and Esther both reflected on the difficulty of distinguishing between "religion" and "cult," though a scale of intensifying control seemed key. As Darren explained, "I would define it by control. I think that's the main thread between any group—[where it falls] on a spectrum of control. And cult maybe [would be] defined as the more extreme point on that spectrum of control."[28] Similarly, Esther noted there was "no hard and fast distinction" between religions and cults, but a cult signified a more amplified and intense form of religious control and authoritarianism than other religions.[29]

The difficulty of distinguishing between the two led some interviewees to stress cult discourse as pointing to community dynamics rather than to the community as an essentialized entity. Tess had been subjected to an escalating process of boundary violation, emotional abuse, and sexual harassment by her teacher Simon, a married man three decades older than her. For Tess, it was important to understand a cult as a set of patterns of behavior rather than a reified object. As she explained, "I think it's great to talk about [a cult] in terms of dynamics, because then it doesn't other it as something that you are not in. . . . When you say, 'these are the dynamics,' you can see them."[30] Like Tess, most interviewees emphasized structures and patterns of behavior as key to understanding what made a specific group a cult. These dynamics were intensified across a "cult scale," and they also cut across different contexts. Jo, a Buddhist teacher who had been subject to sexual exploitation by two spiritual teachers as well as what she described as "emotional incest" with a Buddhist teacher, was drawn to the concept of a "soft cult" that stretched the parameters of cult dynamics to include abusive families and political cultures.[31] Molly, a survivor of abuse in the Shambhala community, echoed this wide parameter. In her words, "Cults can happen anywhere . . . in business, in offices; it's not just a religious thing. It's more of a human organization thing."[32]

Rachel reported that she had been raped while unconscious in the shrine room by her Vajrayana teacher and shunned by her community when she sought help.[33] She was very comfortable using the word "cult" to describe her former community but also talked of the range between "a full-blown cult" and a group in which just the inner circle functioned like a cult. She considered whether it might be more useful to develop "a shared language that captures the manipulation and the control and the betrayal experiences" rather than just "a shared word." For Rachel, however, the "identifiable essence" of a cult was "the harm that comes through the lived reality of coercion and indoctrination."[34] While she felt it was important to nuance the term, the lived reality of harm should not be lost. Many interviewees emphasized the effectiveness of "cult" over other terms to convey this harm. Reflecting on alternative terms such as "high control group" or "high demand group," Esther concluded that "cult" was the most effective because "it's a fast way to talk about an extreme power imbalance that is harmful."[35] Similarly, Betty insisted, "I love the name 'cult' because that's what it is."[36] Even Tess, who showed considerable nuance in parsing out the range and limits of the word, also stressed that nonetheless, "It's okay to call a cult a cult."[37]

TYPES OF CULT DISCOURSE

Interviewees engaged with cult discourse to greatly varying extents. On one side, there were three interviewees—Rachel, Sandy, and Jo—who were or had been fairly immersed in cultic studies and the wider cultic subculture; on the other extreme was Molly, who had not read much, though she had found cult documentaries very helpful.

After a deep dive into cult documentaries and memoirs, Rachel joined an online cult recovery group, which she had found helpful. Rachel was a member of the International Cultic Studies Association and had recently attended a conference called "Not Alone: A Conference for Survivors and Helping Professionals," organized by People Leave Cults in Portland, Oregon, which she described as a "very well-curated space."[38] She named a presentation on adult clergy misconduct and the focus on building community as two elements that had particularly impressed her.[39]

Sandy, a former Jehovah's Witness, had gotten heavily involved in "ex-cult" networks as part of her healing from childhood religious trauma. She knew of high-profile figures such as Janja Lalich and Steven Hassan and had enrolled in a religious trauma certification program. Sandy had grown disillusioned, however, by what she dubbed "the ex-cult industry." As she put it, "everyone wants me to join a group, and everyone wants to become a coach . . . and everyone wants to make [a] documentary."[40]

Jo shared that there was a time when she would click on anything online to do with cults and had amassed a large Google folder on cult recovery. Jo had contacted Rachel Bernstein to discuss the possibility of sharing her story on *IndoctriNation*, and while she decided not to do so, she had connected Bernstein to the Heartwood group and was enthusiastic about the small group work Bernstein had done there. Jo added, however, that she had become put off by some of the more "conspiracy"-type material circulating in the cultic studies subculture and had cooled her interest as a result.[41]

Several interviewees had first encountered cult discourse through Buddhist bridge figures Tahlia Newland, a former member of Rigpa who had become as survivor advocate, and Matthew Remski, who has written prolifically on cult dynamics in Buddhist and yoga communities. Darren had left the Tibetan Buddhist community where he had lived for two years after a harmful institutional response to the sexual harassment of a male student by a monastic leader. As we talked over Zoom, he showed me a copy of Newland's *Fallout: Recovering from Abuse in Tibetan Buddhism*, explaining, "It was just so comforting to read it and see all of the experiences that happened at Rigpa reflected in my own experiences." Darren also named Jennifer J. Freyd's concept of DARVO and Alexandra Stein's application of psychoanalytic attachment theory to the relationship between charismatic leaders and group members as the two resources that he'd found most helpful in making sense of his experience.[42] Darren had contacted Stein and found his conversations with her to be of real benefit in his recovery process. He explained that she had taken a "nuanced approach" to help him understand the problematic patterns of his former community. Their conversations had led him to conclude that "I don't in any way think I was in a capital-C cult, but there were certain controlling cultic dynamics that developed within it all."[43]

Tess had attended Matthew Remski's online workshop "Cultic Dynamics in Meditation Spaces."[44] In his work, Remski draws expansively on cultic studies theorists, particularly the psychoanalytic approach of Alexandra Stein and Daniel Shaw, as well as his own lived experience as a cult survivor. Tess found Remski's approach a "helpful framework" for understanding her experience of boundary violation, and she identified Stein's concepts of a "totalistic environment," "fright without solution," and "disorganized attachment" as particularly relevant. For example, as she explained, "Simon, he would do horrific things, but then he would position himself as the one who could resolve it and frame it. And so, I'd just be caught in this 'fright without solution' state all the time. It had a terrible, terrible impact on my mind."[45] Stein's work had also helped Tess make sense of the lack of intervention from other community members. As she continued, "Stein talks about the way your horizontal relationships are cut off or weakened or replaced [in a cult-like environment]—because the vertical attachment to the leader is paramount." She explained that Simon had tried to separate her from other community members by telling her that they were "crazy" or "jealous" of her. She recognized later that he would have said similar things to them about her.[46]

Three interviewees shared that they had found Amanda Montell's *Cultish: The Language of Fanaticism* very helpful. Montell, who is a linguist and a writer as well as the host of a podcast, places language at the core of what makes a group "cultish."[47] Riley, who had experienced what she described as spiritual abuse and spiritual gaslighting from her Zen teacher, shared her own struggles around language. She explained that she had to articulate her complaints in the Buddhist language of the community to be heard, but she felt that the language itself flattened and diminished her complaints. *Cultish* had helped her see how the group language had worked against her both by keeping her from clearly seeing the power dynamics in her community and by preventing her being heard by others when she tried to name these dynamics.

Another focus was on ex-cult recovery models. Taylor told me she had a whole shelf of cult recovery books, and during our conversation, she jumped up to pull out Gillie Jenkinson's book *Walking Free from the Trauma of Coercive, Cultic and Spiritual Abuse* as one she particularly recommended.[48] Taylor had been the personal attendant of a monastic Tibetan teacher in a residential community for nearly a decade, but their relationship had broken down after he had asked her to lie about and cover up some sexually inappropriate behavior. The resultant fallout had seen her lose her home, job, and community. Taylor still struggled to make sense of the breakdown of her relationship with her former teacher. As she continued, "There's this push and pull between the benefit that I got from him, the love that I still have from him, and the harm that he did to me. And it's still extremely confusing."[49] Taylor had found coercive control the most helpful framework to understand her experience because it explained "the hook, the pull, the failure to be able to leave cleanly." She had taken part in a research study by Kate Amber, the founder of End Coercive Control USA, and she forwarded me emails she'd sent to a lawyer she'd worked with in which she enthused about Amber's model.[50]

As discussed earlier, coercive control is recognized as a crime in some countries. Tess had been able to access the outreach services at a local Women's Aid group after contacting them about Simon's abusive behavior. However, when she looked into taking legal action against Simon, a solicitor informed her that the laws on coercive control would not help her because they only covered domestic relationships and were not applicable to teacher-student relationships—despite the fact that she had shared a residence with Simon.

Several interviewees referred to "spiritual abuse." Only one, however, connected this to a specific reference. Hannah shared that reading an essay on spiritual abuse by Jungian therapist and author Demaris Wehr was a turning point for her in escaping a long-term abusive relationship with her Zen Buddhist teacher.[51] Others used "spiritual abuse" as a generalized term to describe the ways that they had experienced Buddhist doctrine being used for harm or as an obstacle to effectively stopping harm. Riley, for example, shared that Buddhist doctrine "was directly used against me. That was the spiritual abuse part of it. Where it showed up in the container of dokusan—which is, you know, the face-to-face teachings [in] Zen—[and] how the teachings were applied to me were piling on harm and shame."[52]

Finally, all interviewees emphasized how helpful cult documentaries had been to them. For Rachel, cult documentaries had become "part of the soundtrack of my life for a while" and a key part of her starting her healing journey.[53] Virginia shared that she didn't think there was a cult documentary she hadn't seen.[54] While she had not been drawn to cult literature, Molly had watched a lot of documentaries as she found them "very helpful to understand the power dynamics and the pull of these groups." She was wary, however, of the "really sensationalist ones."[55]

"IT WAS LIKE THE PUZZLE PIECES WERE STARTING TO SETTLE AND GET CLOSER": NAMING

All interviewees emphasized that the primary function and value of cult discourse was that it gave them the language to name deeply confusing and harmful experiences. It enabled them to recognize that what had seemed to be an individual experience was actually a shared one with distinct, identifiable patterns across different contexts. This naming often landed with an intense affective impact. Rachel, for instance, talked about the impact of a documentary called *Holy Hell*, which was made by former members of a spiritual group called Buddhafield whose founder and teacher was accused of sexual coercion by a number of male students.[56] "I must have watched that documentary forty times," Rachel exclaimed. "Maybe you'd think, 'how could someone even watch this more than once?' Because it's, like, tragically sad. It's a devastating story of what happened to the people in this cult. But I found it so relaxing. It was so cathartic." She continued, "It was like the puzzle pieces were starting to settle and get closer. . . . The cult content was putting words and narrative onto the same feelings that I was grappling with."[57]

After Jo supported a female student who made a complaint of sexual harassment against their male married teacher Neil, he began to target her. During this "devastating" time, "a friend referred me to Matthew Remski's book *Practice and All Is Coming*. And I saw the patterns and [I thought,] 'Whoa, this is really what's happening here.' . . . I think it was the first time I really kind of admitted to myself, 'I have a history of this,' and Neil was just the cherry on the top."[58] Jo herself had been sexually exploited by two previous spiritual teachers under the pretense of religious practices but had previously thought of them as discrete traumatic life experiences. Placing them within a structural framework of cultic dynamics was the start of a deep healing process for her.

Taylor lost her teacher, work, and community. She was, in her words, "ostracized, blacklisted, [and] not just abandoned, but shunned." Cult discourse gave her a vocabulary to articulate her experience. In her words, "the language of cultic studies is very powerful and can be used to explain what happens to people like me." She described the realization that she was in a coercive relationship with her teacher as "hitting her [in] the belly like a battering ram."[59] Even those who were already intellectually familiar with concepts such as spiritual abuse and gaslighting described a powerful affective moment when they realizing this was what was happening to them. As Riley explained, "I was like, 'Oh! That is what gaslighting feels like! Oh my god, that feeling of fog and slipperiness in that conversation, that is misogyny and patriarchy! That's what it feels like in my body.' And so literally I came to it from in my body."[60]

"I ACTUALLY DON'T THINK I WOULD BE AS FAR ALONG IN MY RECOVERY": HEALING

For survivors of these environments, recognizing that they had been in a cult or cultish situation alleviated a sense of confusion, dysregulation, and shame that they carried. Both Betty and Taylor shared the intense relief they experienced on realizing their situation was not their fault: that they were victims of abuse. Through exploring the structures undergirding coercive control in therapy with Bernstein, for instance, Betty experienced freedom from a crushing sense of self-recrimination. As she explained, "Instead of just blaming myself, I could see that when you get into the machinery, it's difficult to get out. And . . . I mean, yes, I can say I was a victim, but I also became a perpetrator, because that's just the way the system works, because [when] you want to belong, you do the same thing. You make somebody an outcast because they spoke up."[61]

Taylor also explained how understanding she was a victim of an abusive relationship brought tremendous psychic relief. As she explained, "Before, I had been making all sorts of excuses and thinking this was my fault, that I wasn't good enough, that I wasn't faithful enough, that my devotion wasn't strong enough, that this was all on me. And [my teacher] was reinforcing all of this. He was actively saying things like, 'Don't you have enough faith in me? If you had enough faith in me, you wouldn't be experiencing these things that you're experiencing.'"

Another aspect to the recovery process was recognizing the distinctiveness of the harm of being in a cultic group and the need for a therapist who specialized in cult recovery. While all interviewees emphasized that they had benefitted from regular therapy, several experienced exhaustion at having to educate their therapists. Rachel shared that she had found it "very challenging to catch them up to speed."[62] Taylor echoed her, explaining that while her therapist was kind and tried to understand, "it was going to be really hard for her to understand why I had stayed. And I was going to be spending an awful lot of time trying to help her understand why I had stayed and not bailed. And I couldn't go through that again."[63]

As Jo explained, cult recovery therapists "know the degree of what you've been through, whereas another therapist might just equalize it with other traumas." Jo was enthusiastic about the impact of Bernstein's small group, saying she had seen "definite progress" and growth for the women in it.[64] For Rachel, cult content in general provided crucial navigation for those like her leaving abusive communities, especially when there were few other resources available. She ended our interview by expressing tremendous gratitude for cult discourse. As she put it, "There's just no way to express how grateful I am . . . because had I not had that content to consume, I actually don't think I would be as far along in my recovery."[65]

"IT'S LIKE SEEING A RED TRIANGLE ON THE ROAD": WARNING AND PREVENTION

Several interviewees expressed a desire to warn other individuals about harmful groups and also to help reform communities in the wake of abuse by addressing cultic dynamics within them. One reason Betty found "cult" such a powerful word was because she felt it acted like a clear warning sign. As she evocatively put it, "It's like seeing a red triangle on the road, and you know, 'Okay, we have to be careful.'"[66] Hannah echoed this. In her words, "I bring 'cult' in because when I say the word 'cult,' it's like [a] high alert. This word is doing the work of 'Oh, you are harmed. There was probably sexual abuse. . . . There may be financial abuse. . . . There was control.' If I say 'high control group,' not everyone gets that."[67]

Betty suggested creating a "cult scale" that could be used to measure communities' cult characteristics and act as a warning and/or harm prevention measure.[68] Tess had adopted Matthew Remski's best practices for communities to avoid falling into cult dynamics, included in his book, among resources she had collected to help her community recover from teacher abuse. Riley shared that she was developing a website that would provide resources to support those who wanted to stay in and reform communities in which they had experienced harm as well as those who had left communities. The website would include cult discourse particularly related to spiritual abuse and gaslighting in a spiritual context.

By revealing what patterns or structures were harmful, cult discourse also functioned as a way for interviewees to clarify and envision what new types of communities they wanted to create and be part of. Three interviewees mentioned only wanting to participate in nonhierarchical communities, naming Heartwood and Alcoholics Anonymous (AA) as the types of peer support group that they felt offered a safe and supportive community space. Sandy shared that she would no longer participate in hierarchical groups or ones in which she felt there was an agenda to "sell you something."[69] Darren discussed how his experience of institutional betrayal had led him to reconnect to his Indigenous heritage and his appreciation for Indigenous ways of sharing power.

"I'M JUST LOOKING FOR A ROOM . . . WHERE WE CAN ALL RELATE": COMMUNITY

A number of interviewees talked about how the deep human need to belong kept people in communities with cultic dynamics. As Molly mused, "It's kind of a home. It's a sort of rigid and stinky home . . . but you do know where you are."[70] Betty also emphasized her deep need to belong. In her words, "I always kind of wanted to belong. That's another aspect of it. I wanted to belong to a community, and so I tried to do whatever it took to belong."[71] Several expressed how difficult it was to leave a community and in some cases to be shunned by former friends. As Rachel explained, "Leaving a religious environment, you're cutting a lot of really deep ties: spiritual, cultural, social. Leaving is so complex . . ." For Rachel, the wider cult network seemed to have provided a new space to build connections around shared experience. For instance, she identified the "in-person community building" element of the People Leave Cults conference as one of her favorite things about it. Reflecting on the conference and also on the process of creating the Heartwood group, she said, "I'm just looking for a room where we all have that same hurt around betrayal, where we can all relate."[72]

Virginia also emphasized that finding cult discourse had helped her to feel less alone and to realize that there were other people she could connect with who had had the same experience as she had. As she explained, "I was pretty much just on my own . . . but then as more cult stuff started coming out over the years . . . it makes you see that your experience wasn't just an individual [one], it was like [a] part of a larger pattern. And there seems to be some feeling of connection with other people who've had similar experiences."[73] Even Sandy, who was the most critical of the ex-cult network of all the interviewees, was nostalgic about the sense of belonging and connection she had felt at one time within it. As she reminisced, "In the communities of people, they'd be like, 'Hey, this documentary is out! Let's watch it and discuss it,' and that was a way that I connected with a lot of people I know now." While Sandy had become disillusioned with the ex-cult scene, she missed the sense of being rooted in a community that could recognize and help her process shared experiences.[74]

"MY EXPERIENCES OF ABUSE AND ENLIGHTENMENT . . . WERE SEAMLESS": RELIGIOUS ANALYSIS

Rather than use "cult" as a way to distinguish legitimate and illegitimate religion, many of my interviewees questioned whether there was a clear line between religions and cults or religious formation and abusive practice. In doing so, they challenged both the demonization of cults as inherently bad—explicit in classic cult discourse—and the reification of religion as essentially good—implicit in consensus scholarship's prioritization of religious freedom and difference. As Hannah put it, "I think 'cult' is just shorthand for 'bad religion,' whereas 'religion' is shorthand for 'good, divine, holy.' . . . Framing something as a cult denigrates the authenticity of a belief system whereas calling it a religion validates and authenticates it. . . . But I think that religious experience—spiritual experience—is much muddier. It's not, like, good or bad. It's a big mix of both."[75]

Hannah joined her local residential Zen center as a college freshman and moved in a few years later. She describes being groomed by her then-married teacher, who was several decades her senior, a process that escalated into isolation and control. In a reflection she wrote later, Hannah questioned whether it is possible to differentiate between real Zen and the "misuse of power hidden in the guise of Zen."[76] She detailed how her teacher legitimated his intrusive behavior through Zen doctrine and practice. As she explained, "That summer was emotional terror (and some physical terror), justified by Zen stories and reinforced in the dokusan room. At the end of it, when I was truly broken, had burned nearly all bridges between myself, my family, and my friends at his behest, and was thus isolated, he made his move." For Hannah, it is difficult to separate "true Zen" from abuse because there was not a distinct period when her Zen practice ended, and the abuse began. She had many deep breakthroughs during her grooming process. In her words, "My experiences of abuse and enlightenment (to use a freighted Zen term) were seamless." Not only was her Zen center "culty" and "abusive," but she also found it hard to distinguish between the conditions that had made abuse possible in her center and the conditions in other groups.[77] For Hannah, "cult" does not serve as a way to demarcate good and bad Buddhism but rather to blur the boundaries between the two and show the close relationship between traumatic experiences and spiritual practice, both of which she experienced as cracking open her conventional egoic self.

During her experience of teacher abuse, Tess also struggled with separating it from normative Vajrayana Buddhist practice.[78] She described how Simon, her teacher, would use Tibetan teachings to justify his behavior and how she herself had internalized this. As she explained, "I thought I could try to understand it in the terms of the dharma. . . . But retrospectively, I think that that was a kind of conditioning by him, you know, because he would really use the Tibetan canon to legitimize his behavior, not just with me, but everyone." Tess's wake-up call came after she learned that Simon had threatened to kill another young woman if she told anyone they had had sex. This cut through the confusion for Tess. As she explained, "Everything fell into place. . . . When you see somebody else has been really hurt and damaged, then it's not about you resolving in your own mind. It's [that] people are being hurt."[79]

While Tess had found Alexandra Stein's work to be very helpful in understanding what she had experienced with Simon, she had not simply swapped cultic frameworks for Buddhist ones. Rather, she found herself wrestling with the slippage between normative doctrine and abuse, Buddhism and cultic frameworks. She pointed out stories within Vajrayana Buddhism in which the beatings of a lama were considered a blessing. She mused, "Can these dynamics be liberatory in any way? Or are they just a means of control that benefit some lads at the very top? . . . It's very bewildering to me, because on one hand, you have nuns or [people] who talk about their strict retreat as being something very beneficial. And then you have others who frame it as emerging from a cult. What is what and what makes them different? I just don't know!"[80]

"I'M SAYING THAT IT'S ALL A CULT": GENDER CRITIQUE

The slippage between cults and religion was particularly notable for interviewees who identified as feminist. As Wongmo explained, "I was passed a list of behaviors that could be indicative of a cult to share with someone else to help them try to understand what they had gone through. And as I read it through, it was, like, pretty shocking because there were very few behaviors that I did not experience or witness in Tibetan Buddhist communities I was part of."[81] Wongmo began to analyze the ways in which patriarchal institutional structures, Buddhist teachings on 'no self,' and normative female socialization to serve others "powerfully combined" to cement male religious power. There was, she continued, a "cult of personality" around the male head teacher in which "people were encouraging each other and rewarding one another socially for delegating all of their life decisions to him."[82] Wongmo's initial shock turned into a more sober conclusion. In her words, "I'm saying that it's all a cult, because communities can and often do end up functioning as cults because of the presence of an ostensibly infallible patriarchal leader with absolute authority whose wishes should be obeyed." For Wongmo, the patriarchal element and the cult element in the community "fed into each other."[83]

Riley had reached a similar conclusion. She emphasized that her identities as a mother, older woman, and feminist were determinative of how she had come to understand her experience of "gendered harm" in a residential Buddhist community. She described being subject to an aggressive misogynistic verbal attack by a male student after expressing concern at how this man was sexually harassing a younger woman at their residential Zen center. After she reported this incident, however, the male head teacher of the community treated it as an interpersonal rather than structural issue, which caused Riley further harm. She saw the structures of cults, patriarchy, and misogyny as tightly interwoven. Her male teacher had held absolute power, and she experienced him using Buddhist teachings against her when she tried to confront him. Riley shared that while several women in the community offered a modicum of verbal support privately, they would not speak out publicly against him. She had come to see these women almost as "abused wives" whose need to belong in the community overrode other considerations. She confided, "It's now hard for me not to view all formal religion as a cult."[84]

The inability to "objectively" discriminate between "cult" and "religion" has led many scholars to argue that "cult" is a meaningless category. My interviewees, however, suggested that the slippage between the two actually tells us something very meaningful about the dynamics of religion—for instance, how trauma and mystical experience can be interwoven as both put pressure on the conventional bounded self and how gendered power dynamics operate on the ground in religious communities. The slippage also tells us how unstable our analytic categories are. As Ḥannah put it, "There's this desire to have all the categories be neat and separate, and not overlapping, and not mushy . . . I have this desire to have it be cleaner. But that is not the experience, you know?"[85]

"I DON'T WANT ANOTHER TOTALISTIC FRAMEWORK": CONCERNS AND CRITIQUES

Notably, as well as affirming its value, many of the Heartwood members were cautious and critical about cult discourse. Nearly all *rejected it as a totalizing framework* and cautioned against imposing it onto every situation. As Jo explained, "When you take one subject and become an expert in it, there is the risk of trying to make that the case every time you see [anything like it]. And I think that cult experts can fall into that." Darren echoed her point, emphasizing that he only drew on cult discourse selectively and with discernment. As he put it, "I'm not interested in becoming, like, a crusader, part of that anti-cult crusader kind of thing." Reflecting on how and why cult discourse could become a totalizing framework for those who had experienced abuse, Wongmo pointed to the deep disorientation one experienced on leaving a religious community and worldview. As she mused, "One of the things about being in Tibetan Buddhism or in a cult is that the narrative is so totalizing. It accounts for everything in your life, right? It organizes it into a system of meaning; everything is given meaning by that narrative. . . . When you're emerging from that, like, you don't know what story to tell anymore. You are kind of struggling and groping to make up a new story. . . . There can be this moment of 'I need a new narrative, like, give me one that explains everything!' And you want a powerful narrative and a strong narrative, and a totalizing narrative, and yes, 'cult' can be used that way."[86]

Many pointed out that cult discourse could be too reductive and erase the *complexity and value* of the group or cult experience. As Wongmo acknowledged, "Where I think it's unhelpful is . . . I think many of us did find things that were useful, psychologically healthy, hopeful, meaningful [in Buddhism]. And once we start labeling it as a cult, it's very hard to remain in respectful relationship to either the sources of wisdom that you were practicing and to your ability to continue to use the practices that you learnt as a resource for your life."[87] Similarly, Tess "couldn't completely throw the Buddha out with the bathwater." She charted her use of cult discourse along a temporal line, noting that it had served a definite purpose in her healing journey but that she had not completely taken it on. As she explained, "It was really good to just kind of kind of laugh and, like, call it a cult for a bit. It was just necessary to do, but it's also very painful. Because the reason why we were there was because we did see validity in the teachings after all, at the heart of it." For her and other interviewees, cult discourse could reduce the complexity of their experience. As she continued, "It doesn't allow for [the fact that] within cults there can still be these incredibly transformative, meaningful experiences."[88] Darren also stressed that it was necessary to have a "more compassionate and nuanced critique of these groups" because they were meeting needs for people that are not being met by "mainstream culture."[89]

While some interviewees experienced cult discourse as empowering, others felt it could be *shaming and victim-blaming*. As Esther bluntly put it, "People are often made to look totally stupid for getting involved in cults."[90] When I asked Molly what she felt was most important for people to know about cults, she emphasized the need to normalize rather than demonize the people who participated in them. As she explained, "It's just people trying to meet deep emotional human needs . . . and that can take you into very strange and unpleasant places. And it can be very hard to understand, especially if you haven't experienced it, but it can happen to anybody."[91] Jo shared that she was careful about recommending cult material to other survivors because it could be shaming for people to feel that they were in a cult. Wongmo echoed this, sharing that a friend who had also left their Buddhist community because of its abuse history was adamantly opposed to Wongmo calling it a cult.

When I asked if Wongmo's friend would recognize a list of characteristics that constituted a cult if she did not mention the word, Wongmo replied, "Yeah, I think she'd be like, yes, yes, of course, of course!"[92] Hannah also critiqued the "victim-blaming" elements of cultic discourse, which portray survivors in negative, stereotyped ways, but praised more recent books and documentaries such as Montell's *Cultish* and *The Vow* for showing that people who get involved in cultic situations are not damaged but actually "optimistic and idealistic." She shared that this more positive representation had helped her deal with some of the shame she has struggled with over her involvement with Zen.[93] Overall, I found that members of the Heartwood Connecting Survivors of Guru and Teacher Abuse group navigate cult discourse reflectively, drawing on it as a useful but not exclusive interpretative framework.

Three interviewees were aware of academic critiques of cult discourse. Darren was particularly concerned with the harm that the term could inflict on minority religion practitioners by essentializing and othering them. As he put it, "There can also be a lot of that kind of bogeyman hunting [in the cultic studies subculture]."[94] Tess also reflected on the way that ethnocentrism could slip into cult discourse, noting that it was much easier to dismiss Tibetan Buddhist communities as cults if one was not ethnically Tibetan and had not grown up with the tradition as the dominant religious culture. Hannah shared that she was aware of the position that "a cult is just a name for a religious group you don't like" and agreed that subjectivity and bias played a role in what religions were labelled cults. For her, there was no clear line between cults and religions, and the term essentially signified a "misuse of power in a way that causes harm" that could happen in any religious context.[95] Even Betty, who was a strong advocate for the term "cult" and cult discourse, emphasized that "cult" was not synonymous with minority religion. As she explained, "The Catholic Church, which is not a minority religion, has these cult characteristics. Yes, absolutely. It's not necessarily just a small minority group. It could be a local mosque. It's more about, like, identifying harmful patterns."[96]

It is relevant to note that many of my Heartwood interlocutors' critiques of cult discourse are also found in Matthew Remski's 2024 book *Surviving Modern Yoga: Cult Dynamics, Charismatic Leaders, and What Survivors Can Teach Us*, a revised edition of his 2019 book *Practice and All Is Coming: Abuse, Cult Dynamics, and Healing in Yoga and Beyond*. While it still advocates for the value of psychoanalytic cult theorists Daniel Shaw and Alexandra Stein's work in illuminating the relational bonds at work in abusive groups, *Surviving Modern Yoga* also includes a detailed critique of cult discourse, which echoes many points raised in consensus academic critiques. Remski acknowledges, for instance, that "cult" is an imprecise analytic term that can artificially separate good and bad religion rather than show harmful patterns occurring across religions and that cult discourse can be victim-blaming, nonreparative, and weaponized by conservative forces.[97]

Remski warns against the ways cult discourse can become a totalizing narrative, but he also affirms the usefulness of cult discourse at particular stages of recovery. In his words, "I believe that cult analysis can be an effective relief tool for people acutely enmeshed in toxic social conditions. . . . It can be helpful for certain people at early stages of negotiating their relationship to a charismatic leader or high demand group. Later on, it can become a blunt object, limited in explanatory power and psychological nuance."[98] Remski also importantly points out the connections between cultic dynamics and forms of structural oppression such as misogyny, racism, and capitalism. As he puts it, "Systemic abuse in groups relates to systemic patterns of oppression in culture."[99] This resonates with the overlap between feminist critiques of patriarchy and cult discourse that a number of Heartwood interviewees articulated.

"WHAT IT'S HELPING SURVIVORS SAY": CONCLUSION

In my interviews and research, I found significant differences between the NRM consensus approach to cult discourse and the usage of cult discourse by survivors of abuse in Buddhist contexts. Whereas the NRM consensus views "cult" as a name for a religious group you don't like, Heartwood members see "cult" is a name for a religious group you experienced harm in. Though the NRM consensus closely links cult discourse with the widely discredited brainwashing theory, notably not one interviewee mentioned brainwashing. Instead, they referred to processes in which one's agency was compromised as coercive control, gaslighting, grooming, or indoctrination. While several identified Alexandra Stein as a particularly helpful theorist, interviewees rarely referred to more classic cultic studies figures, only briefly mentioning Margaret Singer and Steven Hassan. Whereas the NRM consensus approach highlights how "cult" is used against minority religion, Heartwood members stress that cult dynamics play out across and beyond religious contexts. Similarly, while the NRM consensus critiques how "cult" is used to delegitimate certain religious groups and legitimate others, Heartwood survivors blurred the boundaries between cults and religions in a way that brings them more into alignment with scholarly understandings.

Demographic difference should also be noted. While all thirteen Heartwood members had found cult discourse helpful in their recovery process, only three were or had been more deeply embedded within a wider anti-cult network. None of the interviewees were hysterical parents or ex-members seeking to excuse their brief participation in groups. Several had spent decades in their communities. The majority were still involved in Buddhism; three held roles as Buddhist teachers.

Scholars of NRMs have typically used the stereotype of the "bitter and disgruntled" apostate and the atrocity tale as their main analytic framework to interpret cult discourse and allegations of abuse occurring in minority religions. As should be evident, neither model fits with my Heartwood interlocutors. Only two of my thirteen interviewees were connected with the wider anti-cult network in any significant way and one of these two had become disillusioned with what she dubbed the "ex-cult industry."

There was one interviewee, Virginia, who had come to see parts of Vajrayana Buddhism as forms of "black magic." Her condemnation of Vajrayana Buddhism appears to overlap with some of the Evangelical Christian theological counter-cult rhetoric. However, when I noted that counter-cult Evangelicals also use the language of "black magic," Virginia was keen to differentiate herself from them. As she explained, "I don't feel like I have anything in common with their rhetoric at all. I was deeply involved in Vajrayana Buddhism for thirty-five years and understood it intimately in ways that Evangelicals as [a] group never could." She explained that when she used the term "black magic," she was referring to the ritual violence related to wrathful beings within Vajrayana Buddhism, an aspect of the tradition that she felt was not typically understood by western converts. Virginia gave examples of lamas teaching Vajrayana sutras in which women were threatened with Vajra hell if they criticized their lamas. Such verses, she continued, "are not metaphorical. They threaten dissenters with death by plagues, poison, natural disasters, spirit attacks, and violent death." Virginia shared horrific visions that she had had that she understood as "supernatural attacks" from lamas after she disclosed her experience of sexual abuse. She did not condemn all forms of Buddhism but rather discriminated between what she saw as a legitimate early Buddhism and the later "degenerate" form of Vajrayana Buddhism, which "blends Indian Buddhism, Kashmir Shaivism and Bon shamanistic elements." In her words, "Tantric Buddhism is a very dangerous path and at odds with the Buddha's original teaching."[100] While Virginia was not formally connected to any wider Christian anti-cult networks, and had no interest in any alignment with Evangelicals, she had converted to Catholicism and did share that a Catholic priest had put her in touch with another woman who was recovering from an abusive yoga group.

Virginia followed up on our interview by sending me a number of Buddhist studies articles on Vajrayana Buddhism that explored the historic links between Tantric Buddhism and Hindu Shaivism and an article on the "secret consort" practice in which a woman who refuses to participate is condemned to Vajra hell.[101] While some of Virginia's points are valid and substantiated by reputable academic scholarship, her overall conclusion veers into a problematic essentialism by denouncing the whole of the Vajrayana tradition as delegitimate and conflating it with its more violent aspects.

Former Shambhala student Christine A. Chandler's 2017 book *Enthralled: The Guru Cult of Tibetan Buddhism* is one clear example of the atrocity tale in contemporary Buddhism.[102] While there is a documented history of intergenerational sexual abuse in Shambhala, the book slides from sexual abuse allegations to an extreme ethnocentric conspiracy in which Chandler claims there is "a Tantric cult of mass manipulation and thought control, designed to undermine the reasoning abilities of educated westerners, [and] change their values, perceptions and behaviors."[103] Darren was the only Heartwood interviewee who mentioned *Enthralled*. Notably, he heavily critiqued its overblown allegations and its "harmful" othering of Tibetan Buddhism.

While *Enthralled* fits well into the atrocity tale lineage within Buddhist survivor circles, it occupies a fringe position.[104] This does not mean that the serious problems with *Enthralled* should be dismissed. It is crucial to critique the places in which abuse allegations slide into essentialized ethnocentric and racist claims. This critical work is what the atrocity tale framework alerts us to—the work it does best. It is also important to recognize, however, when the atrocity tale model is and is not a relevant analytic and in what ways it is and is not helpful. Darren expressed a simultaneous concern for *both* the truth of intergenerational abuse in Shambhala *and* for how *Enthralled* weaponized that abuse to cause another form of harm in its demonization of Tibetan Buddhists. He did not feel the need to ignore one form of harm to acknowledge another. Darren's both/and approach contrasts with Bromley, Shupe, and Ventimiglia's suggestion that the *truth* of an allegation in an atrocity tale is irrelevant, and the focus should only be on the *function* of the atrocity allegation.[105]

Rather than the consensus NRM view, my research findings align well with the views of feminist scholars of religion who've raised concerns about abuse in NRMs. Many of my interviewees placed oppressive gender dynamics at the center of their abuse as well as the inadequate and, for many, equally harmful institutional responses to their situation. Some identified explicitly as feminists, referenced feminist theorists such as Audre Lorde, Kate Manne, and Judith Herman, and used feminist terms such as "gaslighting," "DARVO," and "himpathy." As discussed earlier, though feminist scholars' critiques of abuse in NRMs form a distinct lineage from those of the anti-cult movement, there is overlap between the structural analyses developed by both. Similar points of contact appeared in my interviews with Heartwood members, who interwove cult discourse and feminist analysis seamlessly. They drew from both cult and feminist discourses in an effort to name what they had experienced as a structural rather than individualized form of harm.

Another striking parallel between cults survivors/ex-members and survivors of sexual violence is the way both populations have been dubbed as unreliable witnesses and have had their testimonies discredited. In *Tainted Witness: Why We Doubt What Women Say About Their Lives*, feminist scholar Leigh Gilmore examines the cultural processes by which female victims of violence are constructed as less reliable witnesses than men.[106] Gilmore locates the reception of women's testimony in a "long and invidious historical association of race and gender with lying that circulates to this day within legal courts and everyday practices of judgement."[107] Her work analyzes how women—particularly women of color—are considered "unreliable witnesses" and their testimony subjected to doubt, stigmatization, and shame "such that not only the testimony but the person herself is smeared."[108] As Gilmore notes, the discrediting of women, particularly those who are victims of sexual violence, "preexist[s] any specific case."[109] Her analysis of this phenomenon explores the historic and cultural processes by which "women's voices emerge as subject to doubt."[110]

Similarly, in the previous chapter, I showed how the Cult Wars and the construction of the NRM consensus approach as a counter to the anti-cult movement has led to the discrediting of the ex-member as an "unreliable witness" and the primed dismissal of their testimonies as atrocity tales. My interview findings show that this preexisting judgment is inadequate, as Heartwood survivors demonstrated considerable nuance when drawing on cult discourse, including critiquing the limits of the discourse.

This does not mean that scholars should simply accept all that cult survivors say as fact or affirm how they say it without commentary, contextualization, or even critique. As Gilmore states, "an adequate witness is no echo chamber, empty of knowledge and passive in the face of the other's demand, nor is she credulous." Rather, "an adequate witness resists the rush to judgment and learns how to attend to accounts of gendered harm and agency made by impure victims in conditions of complexity."[111]

One way to resist the disciplinary NRM consensus "rush to judgment" is to first determine which types of cult discourse survivors are using and how exactly they are using them and to attend more empathetically to the underlying functions that cult discourse serves for them. As Esther put it, "The important point, though, is that rather than throwing out the word 'cult,' we have to ask what it's doing and what it's helping survivors say. . . . It's a process to go through to be like, 'Oh, that was a cult!' And I can rebuild my life in a way that is filled with healthy relationships . . . and where what I will and won't do are respected boundaries."[112]

CHAPTER 3

From a "Capital-C Cult" to a "Potentially Cultish Culture"

Preventing Harm Beyond the Cult Wars

On March 8, 2025, the popular Buddhist magazine *Tricycle* published an article titled "How to Choose a Sangha: A Writer and Zen Teacher on Discerning Healthy Buddhist Communities from Cultish Enterprises."[1] Written by Zen priest Julie Seido Nelson, the article aims to help Buddhist practitioners discriminate between healthy Buddhist sanghas and those that "may lean towards cultishness." While acknowledging that "cult" is "an unfashionable word," Nelson draws heavily on Margaret Singer's *Cults in Our Midst* to identify the factors that characterize cults, such as an authoritarian leader and techniques of "thought reform." Nelson notes that when used in a healthy way, Buddhist practices "crack our self-centeredness," but in unhealthy contexts, "the chink in our self-centeredness may merely mutate into blind loyalty to an untrustworthy high-control leader." To discriminate between healthy and cultish communities, she suggests a threefold approach: first, to have a clear sense of one's own motivations and ability to maintain healthy personal boundaries; second, to investigate the ethical history of the group, such as whether it has any record of abuse; and third, to test the openness of teachers by seeing how they respond to disagreement and conversations about power dynamics. Such strategies are essential, because, as Nelson puts it, "an ounce of prevention is worth a pound of cure."[2]

Nelson's article is an abridged version of a chapter in her 2025 book *Practicing Safe Zen: Navigating the Pitfalls on the Road to Liberation.* As she explains, she wrote the book after going through a series of "betrayals" in her Buddhist community, the Greater Boston Zen Center (GBZC).[3] After what she names as a clergy misconduct crisis at the GBZC and the resultant community fallout, Nelson and other members developed a survivor-centered resource called the Resilient Sangha Project.[4] It includes a section titled "A Potentially Cultish Culture," which draws on Singer's *Cults in Our Midst* to identify the different ways in which Zen potentially overlaps with cult dynamics.[5] It emphasizes that while GBZC is not a cult, they "have found it useful to consider whether any aspects of our culture could be seen as 'cultish' and, if so, to consider how we might change those aspects of our culture."[6] Also included in the Resilient Sangha Project is a section on Jennifer J. Freyd's concept of DARVO and a statement titled "Why I Stayed: A Message from the Survivor."[7] In the latter, the survivor shares the difficulty of finding words to name her experience of abuse in a religious context. As she explains, "Part of the nature of abuse from a spiritual leader is that it is hard to see from the inside. It's hard to find language for the ways in which things feel wrong."[8] Cult discourse—in this case, Singer's classic cultic studies material and Freyd's more recent DARVO model as well the clergy misconduct model—provided the language to name the harm for the survivor and those in the community who supported her. It also provided the language for those who have remained at GBZC to think about how to prevent potential future harm.

Nelson's article, published in a leading Buddhist magazine with an international readership, her book, which is endorsed by a number of prominent Buddhist teachers, and the survivor-centered website produced by members of the GBZC community show that cult discourse has been adopted in much wider and more nuanced ways than the anti-cult network's use of it alone would suggest. In this final chapter, I survey some recent interventions in NRM scholarship that recognize multiplicity and change within cult discourse and push against the consensus approach. Next, I contrast two approaches to abuse in NRMs: the consensus approach and a structural approach. Finally, I identify some common themes emerging from these interventions and my own research findings and reflect on what they suggest for the future study of abuse and cult discourse in NRM scholarship.

BEYOND CONSENSUS SCHOLARSHIP: NEW TURNS IN THE FIELD

The most recent research on cult discourse comes from British sociologists Aled Thomas and Edward Graham-Hyde's 2024 co-edited collection *"Cult" Rhetoric in the 21st Century: Deconstructing the Study of New Religious Movements*.[9] The collection showcases a range of voices, including senior and junior scholars and perspectives from both NRM studies and cultic studies. While there are a number of essays that represent the consensus approach, it contains three significant interventions. One of these comes from Thomas and Graham-Hyde's cowritten introduction, in which they irrefutably argue that the prevalence of cult discourse in popular culture necessitates a scholarly reorientation within the field of minority religion.[10] Among the arguments they make, two points are particularly relevant for my purposes. One is that Thomas and Graham-Hyde acknowledge that much of the scholarship on minority religion has been shaped by the Cult Wars, and they call on scholars to move beyond these confines. As they point out, "While use of the term is continuously used to delegitimize minority religions, it is important to note its wider uses, which points to more nuanced applications of the term from the moral panics surrounding new and minority religions in the 1970s."[11]

Thomas and Graham-Hyde also push NRM scholars to reflect honestly on how they have treated ex-members as epistemological sources. They note the field is commonly critiqued for its reluctance to "meaningfully engage with the testimonies of ex-members," a reluctance that has "resulted in survivor narratives and instances of abuse being marginalized or muted in the field."[12] They note that NRM scholars have dismissed charges that they are "cult apologetics" but call on them to take the charges more seriously. Thomas and Graham-Hyde ask, "Do these accusations point at an uncomfortable truth for NRM scholars? Does the study of NRMs prioritize the 'insider' experience? Has the field, in its attempt to rightfully combat prejudice and misinformation surrounding certain new religions, allowed the valuable testimonies of ex-members [to] go unnoticed?"[13] Surveying the field, they discover that "rather than maintaining a critical and careful balance from members/ex-member sources," scholarship has "typically swerved hugely in favor of insiders."[14] Thomas and Graham-Hyde point out that while NRM scholars have dismissed outsiders as lacking objectivity, they have not applied the same level of scrutiny to insiders.

Another important contribution in *Cult Rhetoric* is its chapter on the history of Inform, a United Kingdom–based educational charity that was established to provide accurate information on new and minority religious movements in 1988. Written by current honorary director Suzanne Newcombe and senior research officer Sarah Harvey, the chapter reflects on the "dramatically changed" cultural context of Inform since its founding during the time of the Cult Wars.[15] Newcombe and Harvey draw attention to two significant shifts.

The first involves the emergence of new and more legitimate frameworks to understand abuse within religious contexts. One of these is the concept of spiritual abuse, particularly as it has been developed by Lisa Oakley in a Christian context. Newcombe and Harvey emphasize how the concept of spiritual abuse avoids the problematic distinction between illegitimate and legitimate forms of religion, which can be reproduced in classic cult rhetoric. They also highlight how survivors find that the term captures the distinctiveness of the harm they experienced in a religious context. In Newcombe and Harvey's words, "The inclusive framework of harm, covering all religious contexts and particularly more mainstream 'Christian' ones, helps move the debate onwards from the 'cult-wars' in which Inform was founded and helps 'survivors' pinpoint exactly the reasons for their feelings of profound betrayal when abuse happens in religious contexts."[16] Another significant concept is coercive control. They note that while the U.K. government declined to extend the concept of coercive control to religious as well as domestic settings, the patterns of behavior associated with coercive control are now widely recognized. As Newcombe and Harvey reflect, "This can only help those who have been subject to similar pressures in the context of religious and ideological groups."[17] Similarly, they point to how the term "gaslighting," a form of manipulation that occurs within a structure of gender inequity in both secular and religious contexts, has the potential to move the field forward from Cult War fights around the reality of brainwashing.

The second cultural shift that Newcombe and Harvey highlight is the much greater awareness of sexual abuse and harm in mainstream religious contexts compared to when Inform was founded. As they state, abuse revelations against members of the clergy only started to be discussed in the media in the 1980s, but recent years have seen much more mainstream coverage of and state response to abuse across religious contexts.[18] Such revelations, Newcombe and Harvey continue, make it easier to talk about abuse in minority religions without singling out minority religion as the cause of such abuse.

Reflecting on these two cultural shifts, Newcombe and Harvey conclude that the function of cult discourse—in the Anglophone world, at least—has significantly shifted since the Cult Wars period. In their words, while "the idea of 'cult' still serves the interests of authoritarian states which seek to repress ideological dissent, including those associated with groups which are not considered particularly problematic in other contexts . . . [t]he current public discourse around 'cult' in the Anglophone world is less focused on minority religious groups and more generally concerned with harmful patterns of behaviour; this can only be welcome as a way to help individuals in our society be less susceptible to social pressure wherever it is found."[19]

Anthropologist of religion Susannah Crockford also makes a powerful scholarly intervention with her study of how former members of QAnon use the term "cult."[20] Using interviews with former members and qualitative analyses of political journalism and social media, Crockford problematizes the glaring disparity between the utility of the word "cult" for those who have suffered real harm in religious groups and the consensus view within NRM scholarship that the term is meaningless and dangerous.[21] Like Thomas and Graham-Hyde, she also troubles the scholarly distrust of ex-members as unreliable witnesses. As she explains, "Former members are undeniably those with intimate, working knowledge of what groups are like in practice and not just the polished front that may be shown to outsiders."[22]

Taking the accounts of ex-members seriously, Crockford offers two case studies of former members of QAnon—Chae-rin and

Monica, two women in their forties—who both describe a process of descending into what Monica called "madness." Both women neglected their physical and emotional needs and cut themselves off from their social support systems and the wider world as their involvement with QAnon deepened. Chae-rin, for instance, began to stay up all night consuming QAnon content because of a message in QAnon that "those who know, don't sleep," and she described how QAnon members "got rid of their TVs because Q told them not to trust the news."[23] Monica became an admin for a QAnon Telegram channel and would spend eighteen hours a day online. Rarely sleeping or eating, she became increasingly depressed and angry. After each woman questioned some elements of QAnon, however, they were attacked and ostracized by other QAnon believers. Chae-rin was called a "traitor and a Nazi," and her former QAnon friends circulated screenshots of her questions and told others to watch out for her. Monica was doxed and received death threats. Someone broke into her home. Both women were left deeply traumatized by their experiences. Crockford explains that both Chae-rin and Monica found the term "cult" to accurately describe their experience in QAnon: For Chae-rin, it brought "legitimacy and coherence" to her experience and gave her "a route towards healing."[24]

Crockford's empathetic portrayal of the harm Monica and Chae-rin experienced through their involvement with QAnon and her respect for the ways in which they articulate their own lived experience contrasts dramatically with the often generic, faceless portrayal of ex-members as "biased" and "disgruntled."[25] Crockford also notes that while NRM scholars have done much work to dissociate the category of NRMs from violence, there are groups—such as QAnon—that do in fact have violent cultures and that encourage members to perpetrate violent acts. As she notes, "Scholars want to discard the word 'cult' because of its imprecision and negative associations, but it continues to be used because people find few other words to describe a group or movement, political or religious, that they have left because they experienced it as controlling, isolating and violent."[26] In recognition of the term's limits, however, Crockford offers the alternative metaphor of "bubbles"—"containers that are simultaneously isolating, fragile and temporary; secure yet insecure"—to describe the dangers of groups like QAnon and the harm experienced by those who leave them.[27]

Crockford is one of very few scholars to make a case for understanding the value and function of the word "cult" for survivors. She challenges other scholars to consider whom it benefits to say there is no such thing as a cult and calls on them to take more seriously the harm of QAnon and similar phenomena.[28]

American religions scholar Dana Logan has also made an invaluable intervention in her outstanding 2025 article "It Was Never About the Snakes: Synanon, Cult, and the Devil in Religious Studies." Logan uses the case study of Synanon, a drug rehabilitation community that later transformed into a religious community, to trouble the discrediting of cult survivors and challenge the consensus approaches to cult discourse.[29] Synanon was originally founded by Charles E. Dederich in 1958 as a treatment program for addicts. He adopted techniques derived from military experiments with brainwashing and resocialization to develop treatment modalities such as "The Game"—an abusive ritual designed to break people down until they submitted to group authority. Synanon also practiced forms of spatial containment, which developed from its early emphasis that the addict must be separated from friends and family to the implementation of intermittent lockdowns called "going on containment," in which no one was allowed to leave its residential compounds.

In the 1960s, Synanon began to recruit people with no history of drug addiction, and it became a residential community for both drug addicts and non–drug addicts in the 1970s. State agencies also began to send adults and minors to Synanon for compulsory treatment. To protect the large revenue it had amassed from its paying members and donations, Synanon lawyers filed as a religious organization. During this period, it adopted controversial practices such as mandatory vasectomies and head shaving. Its core treatment modalities had already become the most popular model for drug abuse treatment centers, and even after the decline of Synanon as a religious organization, federal drug policy during the neoliberal 1980s encouraged the large network of rehab facilities to adopt its approach. Drawing on the research of ethnographer Kerwin Kaye, Logan shows that the Synanon-derived treatment model, which dominates the criminal justice system's approach to addiction, embraces authoritarian control and enforces an authoritarian system of normative morality that seeks to alter the entire personality of "the addict." As Logan argues, "Synanon matters for religious studies because the group and its offshoots define a historically specific form of religious coercion that is inextricably linked to being resocialized and spatially contained."[30]

Since 1971, former members of Synanon, including children raised in the community, have accused the group of brainwashing and abuse, and journalists have labelled it as a cult due to its abusive therapeutic methods. In Logan's words, "cult" is used here to signify "a kind of bad therapy that used group pressure to brainwash people."[31] Synanon's offshoots have received similar allegations. In 2021, for instance, journalist Rachel Aviv published an article on Teen Challenge, an unregulated Christian boarding school that adopted Synanon methods of control and coercion.[32] Residents of the program described its practices as abusive and called it "kind of a cult."[33] While NRM scholars have dismissed comparisons between brainwashing and NRMs by pointing out that members of NRMs are free to join and leave these groups, Logan points out this is not true for Synanon offshoots. As she states, "No one actually joins Teen Challenge (nor do people who are on probation join treatment centers): you are forced to go there and then kept there until you become a new person. In other words, in this historical and institutional context, brainwashing is not just fake science. It is fake science that has been used as inspiration for institutional practice."[34]

Logan's superb article makes several key interventions in the study of cult discourse. One is to challenge the scholarly consensus that the use of the word "cult" is always dehumanizing. Logan notes that many scholars of American religion, such as Robert A. Orsi and Jonathan Z. Smith, have warned against the label "cult" because of its dehumanizing impacts. Writing on Jonestown, Smith, for example, argues that the job of historians of religion is to reveal the "ordinary humanness" of groups that others call cults and show the continuity between good/legitimate and bad/illegitimate religion.[35] Orsi is concerned with how "cult" defines a group by its aggressive rather than valuable aspects and also how it is used normatively to distinguish between good and bad religion.[36] Logan points out, however, that former members of Synanon use the term in much more nuanced ways than scholars claim, ways that capture rather than flatten the complexity of their experience in Synanon. Take, for example, former member Larry Kronish's response to the question of whether Synanon was a cult. Kronish replied, "The truth is complicated. . . . Did Synanon save my life? Yes. Was it a wonderful place to be? Yes, it saved my life, and I do not regret being there. Did Synanon betray me and wound me? Yes, it is all true. Was it one thing at one time and one thing at another time? Yeah. That's what makes it so fucking difficult. . . . Did Synanon do terrible things? Did it hurt people? Did it injure people? Did it perform criminal acts? YES. Was Synanon an enlightened community that thank God was on the face of the earth, this marvelous thing happened? YES. Was Synanon a cult? YES."[37] As Logan comments, Kronish's understanding of a cult did not dehumanize himself or other members of the community but rather pointed to the ambiguity of their experiences, which included both beneficial and harmful aspects.

Logan also not only takes an implicit survivor-centered approach in affirming ex-members' description of Synanon as a cult but goes further by providing historical context to support their testimony. As Logan eloquently puts it, "The word 'cult' is a heuristic for tracking the specific unfolding of hurt. Affirming people's use of the word begins a search for more information, more historical connections, a better sense of what people hoped that good religion, good care, and good community could have been, and, for the Religious Studies scholar in particular, a willingness to engage in the not-always-religious ethical projects at stake. I affirm that, when C.A. Wittman calls Synanon a cult, she is describing how the organization used the Cold War fantasies of resocialization through torture as a blueprint for ritual life."[38] Logan issues a challenge to historians of American religions to overcome their reluctance to make normative judgments about what counts as good and bad religion and to both name and explain the harm that is caused by cults or religions that were designed to hurt. As she explains, scholars have an ethical responsibility to provide "a denser web of historical explanation: why did they get hurt, in that way, at that time?"[39]

In providing such historical context, Logan offers an alternative genealogy of cults to the consensus NRM approach, which argues that the term always functions normatively to police racial and sexual difference.[40] Logan acknowledges that in cases such as the International Society for Krishna Consciousness (ISKCON) and the Peoples Temple, cult discourse was loaded with racialized concerns and moral panic. But she points out that in the case of Synanon, "cult" was used differently, as a way to signify a form of ritual abuse and bad medical care. She gives the example of a 1971 *New York Times* op-ed in which psychologist Bruce L. Maliver expresses concern about the lack of medical training, licensure, and regulation in Synanon after the suicide of a young woman in a Synanon group. Maliver labels Synanon a cult because of its adoption of potentially harmful psychological treatment modalities, not because of racial difference or unorthodox sexual practices. Similarly, in the autobiographies of children who grew up in Synanon, "cult" is used as a way to describe its intentionally designed abusive rituals. These charges against Synanon occurred before the cult panic around ISKCON and the Peoples Temple. While not entirely separate from these usages in that it still denotes a form of bad religion, the term "cult" when applied to Synanon does not function in the same way. As Logan continues, "Cult, as both a temporally specific and normative assessment in this context, means a group that uses state infrastructure to trap people and control them through ritualizing Cold War social scientific principles of resocialization."[41]

ABUSE IN NEW RELIGIOUS MOVEMENTS: CONSENSUS VERSUS STRUCTURAL APPROACHES

As discussed earlier, Ashcraft acknowledged the dearth of research on abuse in NRMs in his 2018 book *A Historical Introduction to the Study of New Religious Movements*.[42] In 2021, the New Religious Movements Unit at the American Academy of Religion (AAR) annual conference offered a panel titled "Identifying, Naming and

Treating Harm in New Religious Movements."[43] The panel was composed of five participants: Erin Prophet, a religious studies professor; Susan Palmer, a sociologist of religion; Jeff Levin, a professor of epidemiology and population health; Jessica Pratezina, a PhD student focused on child and youth care and sociology; and Brett Merrill, a clinical psychologist and professor. Each panelist began with an opening statement of around five to ten minutes, and an extended question-and-answer period followed. Remarkably, not one panelist identified themselves as working directly with survivors of abuse in NRM contexts. Not one included the perspective of a survivor of abuse in NRMs or discussed specific case studies of abuse in NRMs in their opening remarks. In fact, the perspectives of ex-member were not considered at all, and the panelists gave the impression that nearly all allegations against NRMs came from ignorant or hostile outsiders. Levin, for instance, noted that "we may think we can identify real cases of abuse, but this can be an outsider's conceit."[44] This ignores the numerous allegations of abuse made by former members, including children who grew up in NRMs.

Moreover, over the course of five presentations there were only very brief references to abuse in NRMs and many documented allegations of abuse in groups that were mentioned were ignored or minimized. Prophet, for instance, acknowledged "the case of NXIVM, which many people are familiar with, you know, the quite heinous case of abuse involving branding of women," but did not give any further details, as she seemed more concerned with how abuse within NXIVM would be used to discriminate against other religious minorities. In the question-and-answer period, Prophet noted that in yoga groups, "there are of course well-documented cases of sexual abuse by leaders" but that one man had claimed Iyengar yoga was abusive because "his back was hurt during a yoga class." She countered that she had an issue with this because she herself was a practitioner of Iyengar yoga, and "it has been very helpful to me from a health perspective." What she failed to add was that high-profile Iyengar yoga teacher Manouso Manos had faced multiple allegations of sexual assault since the 1980s but that the organization, including its founder B. K. S. Iyengar, had reportedly failed to address these allegations effectively.[45] After mounting public pressure, the organization investigated the allegations against Manos and publicly revoked his teaching license in 2019.[46] Prophet also naively claimed that while people had been "hurt and injured" in Buddhist communities, such communities had now reformed and that it would "be just wonderful if we could see more bridge building rather than accusation, blame, and lawsuits."[47] In fact, it has only been the threat of legal action and public media exposure that has forced Buddhist communities into addressing abuse allegations, often occurring over decades, against founding and leading teachers.[48]

For her examples of encountering harm within NRMs, Palmer discussed the case of a child being unhappily separated from her father when he went to work in Japan for the Children of God and a woman in the Rajneesh community who had decided to have her fallopian tubes tied so she could be a sannyasin even though she wanted to have children. Strikingly, she did not mention that David Berg, the founder of the Children of God, had encouraged sex between adults and children or that in 2005, Berg's adopted son Ricky Rodriguez murdered his former nanny and then killed himself, having left a message alleging he and others in the group were sexually abused as children.[49] A number of other former members of the Children of God have also publicly alleged they were sexually abused in the community as children.[50] Nor did Palmer mention that the Rajneesh community imploded in Oregon after several senior members plotted to poison the local population, and one of these, Ma Anand Sheela, was subsequently jailed for attempted murder and assault.[51] A number of adults who grew up in the Rajneesh community have also revealed that they were sexually abused as children in a heavily sexualized culture of complicity. In fairness to Palmer, such accounts were only published after the 2021 panel; however, given her ignoring of sexual abuse within the Children of God, one is left with little confidence that she would have addressed these reports either.[52]

Levin made a brief comment about Gwen Shamblin and the Remnant Fellowship, noting that "if you read some of the court testimony, it does seem pretty awful, but nobody was ever convicted of anything."[53] He did not add that in 2007, two members of the Remnant Fellowship, Joseph and Sonya Smith, were sentenced to life in prison plus thirty years for beating their eight-year-old son, Josef, to death as a punishment. The Remnant Fellowship supported the couple and contributed financially to their legal defense. Though no legal charges were brought against the Remnant Fellowship itself, a number of former members suggested the culture of Remnant influenced the Smiths.[54] Levin also praised Scientology's detox program—without any mention of the numerous legal battles they have fought with former members who have accused them of abuse.

Pratezina, to her credit, did acknowledge that a lack of convictions did not mean abuse was not occurring in NRMs but gave no details of such abuse. She focused rather on the harm caused by separating children from parents in the 2008 raid on the Yearning for Zion Ranch, run by the Fundamentalist Church of Jesus Christ of Latter-Day Saints (FLDS) community. The raid was based on what was later discovered to have been a false accusation. However, Pratezina did not add that eleven FLDS members, including leader Warren Jeffs, were convicted on child sexual assault, underage marriage, and bigamy charges, nor did she include the testimony of any of the victims, among whom were a fifteen-year-old girl and a twelve-year-old child. There was no consideration of the role that the theology and gender norms of the FLDS played in these crimes against children.[55]

Merrill did not mention anything about abuse in NRMs specifically but rather discussed the experiences of LGBTQIA+ Mormon students at Brigham Young University.

Notably, none of the panelists referenced discussions within the field of NRM scholarship about its lack of attention to abuse, as Ashcraft recognized, or concerns raised by feminist scholars such as Jacobs over the silencing of their analyses of abuse in NRMs. There was no discussion of any shifts within cult discourse, such as the emergence of the spiritual abuse model or the criminalization of coercive control, though there were references to classic cultic studies experts such as Steven Hassan and deprogrammer Ted Patrick.

Rather, the panelists focused almost exclusively on the ways in which abuse allegations and convictions had been weaponized to discriminate against NRMs and on levelling critiques against the "global anti-cult" movement. While Pratezina raised some important points about the need for religious literacy among state agencies to better serve victims of abuse in NRMs, the panelists gave little attention at all to testimonies of survivors of abuse in NRMs and provided no analysis of the ways that structural factors such as doctrine or leadership models within NRMs might increase the likelihood of abuse and prevent effective responses to it. In short, nearly thirty years after the Cult Wars climax of the 1990s, the 2021 AAR panel reproduced the consensus NRM approach of centering minority religions over attending to survivors of abuse within them. As such, the panel would have been much more aptly titled

"Identifying, Naming and Treating Harm *Against* New Religious Movements."[56]

Sarah Harvey's groundbreaking book *Abuse in New Religious Movements* forms a striking contrast to the 2021 AAR panel.[57] A research product of the survivor-centered Abuse in Religious Contexts project, it is structured into three sections. The first section provides a historical overview of how abuse has been treated in NRM scholarship. In it, Harvey makes several main points. Firstly, she notes that NRM scholarship on abuse has been largely shaped by its opposition to cultic studies; while NRM scholars are "generally skeptical" of ex-member accounts, cultic studies prioritizes them.[58] She also raises the sociological method of triangulation as a third option, one that attempts to produce a more "objective picture" by including multiple perspectives on a group. Harvey affirms her disciplinary commitment to the triangulation approach, but she crucially acknowledges that this research is "part of a survivor-centred project; inevitably then, survivor voices and accounts of abuse are prioritised within this Element . . . [which] is an attempt at an intervention and rebalancing within the field."[59] Harvey also agrees with Ashcraft that NRM scholarship has focused too narrowly on lethal violence and argues for a wider understanding of abuse than has been previously employed in NRM scholarship, stating that she has used the definition of abuse from the Abuse in Religious Contexts project.[60]

In the second section, titled "A Theoretical Model of Abuse: Structural and Cultural Factors," Harvey offers a nuanced theoretical framework for understanding abuse in NRMs, which is based on an analysis of around two hundred NRMs that had been marked with the theme of abuse on the Inform database. The model consists of six structural, organizational factors and six cultural, belief- and practice-related factors that can lead to abuse, the legitimation of abuse, and prevent abuse from being addressed.[61] The six structural factors are isolation, leadership, membership, blurred boundaries, education, and health. The six cultural factors are unequivocal beliefs, gender, sex, purification, punishment and pressures, and leaving and shunning. Harvey emphasizes that these are risk factors rather than predictive factors and differentiates them from cult characteristics on the grounds that they occur across religious settings. In her words, "These aspects can be found across all forms of religious movements, as survivor testimonies from those who have experienced abuse in the Anglican and Catholic church highlight."[62] She does note, however, that some factors are closely connected to the culture of NRMs specifically, namely, separation from society, charismatic leadership, and the enthusiasm of first-generation converts, which has consequences for members' willingness to submit to authority. As she explains, the culture of NRMs can intensify these some of these factors even though they are not unique to NRMs.

The third section of Harvey's work applies the structural model developed in the second section to the Jesus Fellowship Church (JFC), a United Kingdom–based Evangelical movement that began in the 1960s and closed in 2019, largely due to abuses that had taken place within it. As Harvey notes, women, children, and men were victims of abuse, and seven members of JFC were convicted of sexual assault on other members, most of whom were minors. The abuse was widespread and systemic: The police received over two hundred allegations of abuse, including sexual, physical, and emotional abuse. In addition, many members reported being adversely impacted by witnessing such abuse. Harvey notes that the experiences of members fitted well with Oakley's model of spiritual abuse.

In her conclusion, Harvey notes that abuse can occur in any context—religious or secular—in which there are hierarchies of power as well as other structural and cultural factors that can increase the risk of abuse and prevent effective responses. Yet she also identifies elements that are unique to religious contexts: a leader, text, or tradition that represents a metaphysical force and therefore carries a distinct authority. Harvey aligns her position with Oakley's concept of spiritual abuse, which suggests that there is something unique about abuse that occurs in religious contexts.[63] As Harvey explains, "The metaphysical dimension adds an additional layer of authority, has an effect on the individual's metaphysical frame of reference and can contribute barriers to the movement's propensity to change and to eradicate harmful dynamics and practices."[64] While Harvey emphasizes that spiritual abuse occurs across religious contexts, she adds that certain factors in NRMs, such as the enthusiasm of converts and isolationist tendencies, can be "conducive to the perpetration and concealment of abuse."[65] She ends by calling for greater dialogue between NRM studies and cultic studies and by recognizing the need to situate the study of abuse in NRMs within the wider turn in religious studies scholarship to address abuse across religious contexts.

Harvey's book is exemplary and provides a much-needed compass for redirecting the study of abuse in NRMs. Several contributions in particular should be highlighted. Harvey takes a survivor-centered approach that works with a wider of definition of abuse that is aligned with feminist analyses of gender and sexual violence, and she also acknowledges the central role that teachings on sexuality and gender have played in abuse in NRMs, a perspective that also aligns more with feminist rather than consensus approaches. With these foundations, she develops a nuanced structural framework that avoids both the essentialism that has marked much of cultic studies and the minimization or ignoring of abuse that has marked consensus approach within NRM scholarship.

RETHINKING ABUSE AND CULT DISCOURSE IN THE STUDY OF NRMS: MOVING FORWARD

Drawing from my own research findings and the invaluable contributions of the scholarship discussed above by Thomas and Graham-Hyde (2024), Crockford (2024), Newcombe and Harvey (2024), Logan (2025), and Harvey (2025), I suggest that the following shifts are necessary to reorient scholarship on abuse and cult discourse in NRMs:

1. Taking survivors of abuse in NRMs seriously as epistemological sources
2. Acknowledging shifts within cult discourse and demographics
3. Replacing predetermined theoretical frameworks with more empirically based understandings of power
4. Situating abuse in NRMs in the wider context of abuse in religion

1. TAKING SURVIVORS OF ABUSE IN NRMS SERIOUSLY AS EPISTEMOLOGICAL SOURCES

A number of scholars have problematized the discrediting of ex-member testimony in NRM consensus scholarship. This discrediting is inextricably linked to the lack of attention to abuse that has characterized this field of study. It is notable that the one book that is dedicated to a structural analysis of abuse in NRMs, Harvey's *Abuse in New Religions*, is a product of a survivor-centered research project. To take abuse seriously in any context—religious or secular, majority or minority religion—it is evident that survivor testimony has to be centered. In his work with survivors of sexual abuse by Catholic clergy, Catholic historian Brian Clites has advocated for academics to take a survivor-centered approach, pointing out how survivor activism paved the way for subsequent scholarly interpretations of the Catholic sexual abuse. As he explains, "I know from my ethnographic work just how robustly survivors contextualize their own abuse, and I often marvel at their critical awareness of the broader cultural dynamics at play in debates about the causes and meanings of clergy abuse."[66] In a similar vein, many of my Heartwood interlocutors and former Synanon members such as Larry Kronish offer valuable and incisive observations into the complex nature of religious experiences and the dynamics of abuse in religious settings. Scholars' dismissal of these insights because of a blanket rejection of cult discourse represents a failure to respect the agency and abilities of survivors as interlocutors and co-knowledge producers in areas of religious abuse.

A key part of taking survivors seriously as epistemological sources is not immediately rejecting the language they use to describe their experiences. In their cowritten book on spiritual abuse, Lisa Oakley and Justin Humphreys emphasize that it is vital to include survivor voices when developing analytic models and to respect how survivors choose to name their experiences.[67] In chapter 1, I argue that instead of constraining survivors' usage of certain terms, scholars should rather ask questions about the meaning, function, and value of those terms for survivors. In her research, Logan suggests that scholars should not only affirm the ways in which cult survivors describe their experiences but also fill out the picture by providing historical context for their experiences. As she puts it, "'Affirm' is a funny word: it is not a creedal 'I believe'—but it is an acknowledgment of the contextual truth of another's experience. In the case of the young women trapped by Teen Challenge, affirming means doing the historical legwork inspired by their intuitions about what was happening to them, which, importantly, they do not know themselves."[68]

Logan troubles the disjuncture between the "recent and necessary cultural acknowledgement that we need to believe survivors of abuse" and the fact that "religious studies tells our students not to believe survivors in podcasts, documentaries, and memoirs who tell us they belong to a cult."[69] One benefit of taking a survivor-centered approach toward cult discourse is that it brings this population more into conversation with feminist approaches to sexual violence. This is crucial given both that the main victims of sexual violence are women and girls and that gender and sexuality are central to abuse in NRMs. Three of the six cultural factors that Harvey identifies in her structural model of abuse, for instance, are related to gender and sexuality, and her specific analysis of the Jesus Fellowship Church shows that patriarchal control was a dominant factor in abuse.[70]

As Harvey states,

> Gender-based abuse or violence, abuse perpetrated against another person because of their actual or perceived gender, is more likely to be experienced by women and girls, who are generally more at risk of domestic violence, rape and sexual abuse, and honour-based abuse. Women are also more likely to be victims of gendered techniques of abuse such as coercive control (Stark 2007; Anderson 2009) and gaslighting, which employ tactics that "are gendered in that they rely on the association of femininity with irrationality" (Sweet 2019: 851). These forms of gendered abuse are found in families where religion may be a factor in the domestic abuse of women and children (Nason-Clark 2000, 2003; Afzal and Stiebert 2024), and/or they can be played out in the dynamics of religious leaders and followers or among peers in religious movements.[71]

In chapter 2, I discussed how both cult survivors/ex-members and survivors of sexual violence have been dubbed as unreliable witnesses and had their testimonies discredited. Roderick P. Dubrow-Marshall argues that cult discourse functions as a way to call out systemic abuse and coercion in groups in parallel to the way that terms such as "domestic abuse" or "rape culture" function call out the systemic abuse and coercion of victims of sexual abuse or gender violence.[72] He also notes that both sexual abuse and domestic violence researchers as well as cult researchers include the emic perspective of the survivor as a core methodological commitment and focus on action-based research that directly impacts the lives of research populations.[73]

It is also notable that feminist scholars of religion were the first to produce analyses of abuse in NRMs and to theorize this abuse as a microcosm of the wider climate of patriarchy and misogyny in society. More research is needed on the overlaps and differences between cult discourse and feminist analyses of gender violence and sexual abuse. Such research can point to the ways in which feminist structural analyses can better inform and refine cult discourse and critique forms that veer into problematic essentialism.[74]

2. ACKNOWLEDGING SHIFTS WITHIN CULT DISCOURSE AND DEMOGRAPHICS

In *Abuse in New Religious Movements*, Harvey identifies the issue of whether certain groups have inherently harmful characteristics (or not) as the point of differentiation between cultic studies and NRM scholarship. She acknowledges, however, that cultic studies has developed beyond its earlier essentialist approach in which cults were by nature harmful. In her words, "Of course, there have also been developments in cultic studies over time and some authors associated with ICSA have also written about cultic properties being on a continuum and as interactionist. Rosedale and Langone (2015) note that because of this definitional ambiguity,

ICSA does not produce a list of cults but rather directs 'inquirers' attention to potentially harmful practices, rather than to a label.'"[75]

Both Thomas and Graham-Hyde (2024) and Newcombe and Harvey (2024) note that cult discourse has extended far beyond the classic theories of brainwashing. Three new models are of particular significance. One is coercive control. As Harvey notes, coercive control is a relatively new area of inquiry in both majority and minority religions. While rejecting the conflation of coercive control with brainwashing, Harvey notes its potential for understanding abuse dynamics in religion. She writes, "I agree that coercive control can be considered a technique or mechanism of (largely gendered) abuse within religious movements."[76]

Another is spiritual abuse, particularly as developed by Lisa Oakley.[77] Speaking from a Christian context, Oakley and Humphreys acknowledge overlaps between cults and spiritual abuse and suggest that when environments are extreme, spiritually abusive churches operate akin to cults. Rather than focus on whether a group is a cult or not, they suggest that it might be better instead to illuminate the types of harmful behavior that can happen in the context of cult or a church.[78] When applied across religious contexts, the concept of spiritual abuse has the potential to avoid the stigmatization that more classical cultic studies frameworks can place on minority religions.

The spiritual abuse model offers a much-needed framework for understanding how religious doctrine, practice, and authority can be mobilized in abusive ways. More research on spiritual abuse within NRMs/minority religions is necessary. Such an investigation should attend to the ways in which spiritual abuse intersects with other forms of abuse. British yoga scholar Amelia Wood has argued, for instance, that it is necessary to expand the conceptual parameters of spiritual abuse to include sexual abuse.[79]

Jennifer J. Freyd's work on institutional betrayal, and in particular her DARVO model, constitutes another helpful resource. DARVO has been adopted by many participants in the wider anti-cult network. It is a model that is not context-specific and so does not essentialize minority religions as inherently harmful. Sociologist Nicole Bedera, the author of *On the Wrong Side: How Universities Protect Perpetrators and Betray Survivors of Sexual Violence* (2024), has appeared on a number of cult podcasts.[80] Drawing on her research and work as a survivor advocate, Bedera discusses how patterns of victim-blaming, protection of perpetrators, and institutional betrayal appear in university settings. In personal correspondence, Bedera clarified that she saw institutional betrayal as the connection between sexual violence within university settings and other contexts. In her words, "I argue that the specific institution doesn't really matter, so long as the victim's social environment—university, church or a cult—meets the parameters of institutional betrayal."[81]

There is also a need for more updated research on the range and type of populations adopting cult discourse. For instance, consensus NRM scholarship depicts those who use cult discourse as being invested in maintaining normative religious and social norms and hostile to racial and sexual difference. Yet cult discourse has also been taken up by populations from marginalized communities. For example, in the Buddhist context, Lama Rod Owens, a queer African American Tantric Buddhist teacher and Buddhist social justice leader, views cultic studies as a helpful framework for understanding sexual abuse in Buddhism.[82] Rachael Reign, the Black British founder of spiritual abuse advocacy organization Surviving Universal UK (SUUK), is an ex-member of the transnational Evangelical Pentecostal Universal Church of the Kingdom of God (UCKG), where she claims to have experienced forms of psychological abuse, spiritual abuse, and labor exploitation, and which she describes using cult discourse.[83] Reign has critiqued UCKG for targeting Black people and has worked to raise awareness in the Black British community of abuse in religious settings.[84] On the other side of the Atlantic, certified trauma recovery coach Nikki G. is a Black American who cohosts *Surviving the Black Church Podcast* and who cofounded the Black Religious Recovery Trauma Network, a resource to educate and empower Black cult and religious trauma survivors. She freely uses cult discourse in characterizing her own experience and in supporting others through theirs.[85]

Cult rhetoric has also been adopted within sex-positive communities. For example, Cara Cordoni—founder of the organization 3SC, which advocates for safer sex-positive and spiritual communities in the United States—draws heavily on cult discourse and was a guest on Rachel Bernstein's cult-focused podcast *IndoctriNation*.[86]

Rather than treat cult discourse as a monolithic entity with the Cult Wars as its sole genealogy, scholars should pay attention to the multiple different lineages and contexts it comes from and circulates within.[87] This does not mean that scholars should stop interrogating the ways in which some forms of cult discourse continue to be employed to target vulnerable minorities, religious or otherwise. Take, for instance, Steven Hassan's ludicrous claim that online pornography and social media groups are hypnotizing young people and brainwashing them into gender transitioning.[88] Hassan's contribution to the moral panic around the transgender movement clearly echoes the anti-cult Satanic Panic of the 1990s and should be critiqued. However, scholars should nonetheless acknowledge that this is only one of a number of uses of cult discourse and that they should not reduce other quite distinct forms and functions of cult discourse to it.

3. REPLACING THEORETICAL FRAMEWORKS WITH NUANCED, EMPIRICALLY BASED UNDERSTANDINGS OF POWER

Consensus NRM scholarship prioritizes the principle of religious freedom and religious difference above all other considerations. Subsequently, it has taken a defensive default stance toward NRMs, typically reifying them as vulnerable victims of state and social violence that necessitate academic protection. While such a position has been helpful in providing insightful analyses of how dominant religious and cultural power operates against minority religions, it has also obscured how dominant power operates within minority religions. It is not always the case, for instance, that minority religions have been targeted by the state. In her account of Synanon, for example, Logan shows that the group's practices have been adopted and supported by the state. She calls on scholars to look beyond the paradigmatic examples of Jonestown and the Branch Davidians because staying with those examples "obscure[s] something real about the use of the word 'cult' in our world (by which I mean the United States since the 1950s)."[89] While NRM scholars replaced the term "cult" with "NRM" to avoid discrimination, Logan argues that, in cases such as Synanon, such a linguistic switch is not only ineffective as an analytic lens but also ethically problematic. As she puts it, "This is a type of group for which the terms 'new religious movement' (NRM) or 'minority religion' hide more than they illuminate because those terms are protective, and some groups—Synanon and Scientology—do not need protecting."[90]

Feminists working on gendered violence and sexual abuse in minority religion in the United Kingdom have raised similar points. One of these is solicitor Pragna Patel, a founding member of Southall Black Sisters (SBS), Project Resist, and Women Against

Fundamentalism, three organizations dedicated to helping Black and minoritized women facing gender-based violence.[91] Patel has written extensively on gender abuse in minority religion and the ways in which U.K. state policies have enabled such abuse.[92]

For example, in her keynote lecture at the 2024 Apostasy Conference, whose focus was the systemic nature of religious abuse, Patel discussed how male authorities within South Asian British minority religions have covered up abuse, with profoundly harmful impacts for women and children, and the ways in which state-based policies such as allowing sharia courts or Sikh courts have facilitated this.[93] Patel argued that the state protects the patriarchal status quo in minority religions in order to procure votes from these communities. She concluded that we must better understand how patriarchal religious authorities represent themselves as guardians of tradition and weaponize principles such as multiculturalism in order to maintain gender dominance.

In the question-and-answer period of Patel's presentation, I asked her what role she felt academics had played in these dynamics. Her response was sobering: Academics have been part of the problem, because like the state, they have often uncritically endorsed patriarchal religious authority in an unnuanced deference to postcolonial politics. Academics have focused on critiquing state oppression of homogenized minorities and failed to interrogate power structures and abuses of power within as well as against these communities. Further, Patel added, conservative patriarchal forces within these communities weaponize academic research on racism and decolonization to reinforce their dominant power.[94] Patel has spent her entire career advocating for Black and Brown minority women in both grassroots and legal contexts. Clearly, she is not ignoring racialized dynamics in gendered violence. Rather, she is problematizing how a unnuanced commitment to a predetermined framework—in this case, an uncritical deference to what she labels as religious identity politics—can actually enable gendered violence to occur.[95]

Yehudis Fletcher, a member of and survivor of sexual abuse within the Charedi Orthodox Jewish community, has also problematized postcolonial feminist academic approaches to abuse in minority religions.[96] Fletcher is the cofounder of Nahamu, an organization that combats culturally specific harms in the Jewish community, such as forced marriage and the covering up of sexual abuse in the Charedi community.[97] She was also an honorary research fellow for the Abuse in Religious Contexts project. Fletcher has written about how her efforts to address gendered violence and sexual abuse in her own community have been met by resistance from both its patriarchal leadership and by progressive feminists who place ideals of "cultural sensitivity" above the lived experience of victims of violence.[98] She explains how conservative apologetics within her own community draw strategically on identity politics and multiculturalism to enforce their oppressive gender policies. These patriarchal forces, she continues, find support from progressive feminists, who often prioritize respecting religious difference above all else. Fletcher argues that the postcolonial feminist dismissal of universal feminist principles as white feminism often results in the consolidation of power for patriarchal oppressive leaders because gender critique is equated with and dismissed as a form of colonial oppression. She concludes, "Feminists are so afraid of 'colonizing' a community with ideas alien to it, that they are content leaving the women inside that community ineligible for the feminist project. What they don't realize is that Haredi Judaism isn't unique or special in the way women within it experience oppression. If you cut us, we bleed. Our patriarchy is as banal and as grinding as yours."[99]

Fletcher's piece shows the importance of starting with the lived experience of victim-survivors of abuse within such communities rather than a predetermined a priori academic framework. American religions scholar Philip Deslippe makes a similar point in relation to his own research into the abuse that occurred in the Healthy, Happy, Holy Organization (3HO) started by Yogi Bhajan, who was revealed in 2020 to have committed abuses against many women and girls in the organization.[100] Deslippe, who had spent a decade as a student in 3HO, found himself in the position of subject matter expert and began to review the academic studies that had been done on 3HO over the previous five decades. He explained, "What struck me the most within all of this writing was how inaccurate most of the academic accounts of 3HO felt in light of all that had just been made public. In the academic monographs, journal articles, and chapters from edited volumes, there was almost no mention of the crime, abuse, fraud, and assault that permeated the group. Some academics who studied 3HO largely relied on their reading of written texts produced by the group and the theories provided by others in their field."[101]

Deslippe met journalist Stacie Stukin, who was writing a piece on Yogi Bhajan for *Los Angeles* magazine, and the two have since cowritten several pieces that have revealed financial exploitation and sexual abuse in 3HO.[102] As Deslippe explained, "Journalism allowed me to do work that felt like a counter to much of the academic work on New Religious Movements I had encountered. Paying meticulous attention to facts and direct testimonies from survivors, instead of academic theory and literature reviews, allowed me to write more freely and definitively on abuse. Unlike academic peer review, which often asks how work fits into currently accepted models and discourse, journalistic editorial review tended to simply ask if something could be factually verified and if I had multiple sources for a claim."[103]

Work by Logan, Patel, Fletcher, and Deslippe shows, from different angles, the limits of approaching abuse allegations in NRMs from the perspective of a predetermined academic framework, whether that framework be protecting religious freedom and religious and sexual difference, multiculturalism, or postcolonialism. Taking a predetermined analytic framework as the starting point of analysis rather than the empirical facts of survivors' allegations can deflect from how power is actually operating in a specific situation and can obscure and thereby enable abusive conditions. For instance, while allegations against minority religions might be understood as reflecting heteronormative bias against unorthodox sexual practices in certain cases, this does not mean that abuse never occurs in communities that practice unorthodox sexuality. Both conflating unorthodox sexuality with abuse and reifying unorthodox sexuality as nonabusive are essentialist and problematic moves. Scholars must do the work of carefully analyzing specific cases of abuse allegations and contextualizing them individually rather than relying on, imposing, and overextending predetermined analytic frameworks such as the captivity narrative or the atrocity tale to dismiss them.

4. SITUATING ABUSE IN NRMS IN THE WIDER CONTEXT OF ABUSE IN RELIGION

Due largely to the media exposure of widespread child sexual abuse in the Catholic Church in the early 2000s, there is an increasing cultural awareness of the reality and extent of sexual abuse in religious contexts. State investigations into child sexual abuse in religion have discovered deep institutional complicity. The Australian Royal Commission into Institutional Responses to Child Sexual Abuse (2012–17), for instance, found that while child sexual abuse occurred in a broad range of institutional contexts, there were more reports of abuse in religious organizations than any other type of organization.[104] The Commission focused on thirty case studies, including majority and minority religions, and interviewed more than four thousand survivors of child sexual abuse. Its findings were sobering. It states that "many religious leaders knew of allegations of child sexual abuse yet failed to take effective action. Some ignored allegations and did not respond at all. Some treated alleged perpetrators leniently and failed to address the obvious risks they posed to children. Some concealed abuse and shielded perpetrators from accountability. Institutional reputations and individual perpetrators were prioritised over the needs of victims and their families."[105] Notably, the report also identified underlying theological and scriptural beliefs and practices as factors in abuse.

While less attention has focused on adult cases of abuse, Dorothy Small, a survivor of sexual assault by a Catholic priest as an adult and a leader in Sacramento's Survivors Network of those Abused by Priests (SNAP), says, "It's imperative to recognize that the prevalence of clergy sexual abuse extends beyond children, impacting adults significantly more than widely perceived."[106] A 2008 Baylor University survey of adult congregants across seventeen Christian and Jewish denominations found that more than 3 percent of women reported experiencing clergy sexual misconduct.[107] A 2015 study by Baylor University researchers interviewed 280 adult female survivors who had filed reports of clergy sexual abuse to their churches.[108] Citing this study, Pooler shared that thirty-nine of these survivors suffered from post-traumatic stress disorder, with many more reporting symptoms consistent with trauma such as disconnection and distrust. He also emphasized that the impact of clergy misconduct was long lasting and that institutional betrayal created a secondary layer of trauma.[109]

In recognition that the power differential between clergy and congregants renders consent by the latter impossible, clergy sexual misconduct is a crime in thirteen states in the United States. In a statement supporting a 2024 bill to make clergy sexual misconduct a legal offense in California, SNAP stated that "clergy abuse of adults not only affects those in the three major Christian groups in the United States, Protestant, Catholic, and Orthodox, but (those) in every other religious community as well."[110] Journalists have increasingly spotlighted the prevalence of adult sexual abuse within yoga communities and other alternative spiritualities.[111]

Alongside increasing public awareness there is a steadily growing body of scholarship on sexual and other forms of abuse in religious settings.[112] Some of this work takes a survivor-centered approach and shows the ways in which religious forms of authority, community, beliefs, and practice are deeply implicated in abuse.[113] For example, in his study of survivors of clergy sexual abuse in Catholicism, American religions scholar Robert A. Orsi emphasizes how this abuse occurred in a distinctly Catholic way. He writes, "'There is no one' among the victims of clerical sexual abuse, a survivor named Monica told me, 'who was not abused in a Catholic way.'"[114] Orsi has called on scholars of religion to honestly confront the harms occurring within religion without minimization or excuse.[115]

While NRM consensus scholarship has primarily approached allegations of abuse through the atrocity tale framework, I suggest that they should follow Harvey's lead and situate such allegations within the broader context of abuse in religious settings. This does not mean ignoring the ways such abuse allegations can interact and have interacted with other forms of violence such as minority religious discrimination, racism, or ethnocentrism. Advocates and scholars working on sexual and related forms of abuse in Islam, for example, have crafted approaches that are careful to avoid reproducing racism or Islamophobia.[116] These provide crucial models to work with. However, as religious studies scholar Rose Deighton-Mohammed notes, while it is essential to acknowledge how stories of abuse are weaponized in service of Islamophobia, Muslim feminists themselves argue that "decentering survivors for the purpose of insulating the broader community from Islamophobia is not an adequate method of response."[117] Indeed, to sufficiently address abuse in NRMs, it is necessary to center survivors of abuse rather than center the religious group in which abuse occurs. Harvey's approach to abuse in NRMs, for instance, was notably shaped by her participation in the survivor-centered Abuse in Religious Contexts project.[118]

CONCLUSION: BUILDING BRIDGES TO PREVENT ABUSE

In his influential 2004 book, *Between Heaven and Earth: The Religious Worlds People Make and the Scholars Who Study Them*, American religions scholar Robert A. Orsi rejects the term "cult" because, among other problems, it defines a religious group by its negative and aggressive rather than positive and valuable aspects.[119] In his later work on the horror and scale of the Catholic clergy sexual abuse crisis, however, Orsi makes something of a countermove by emphasizing not the positive aspects of religion but rather the inextricability of harm from religion. Here Orsi calls on scholars to resist "the power of the idea that religion, in the end, is essentially good," and to acknowledge the harm of religion "before we scramble up toward the warm sunlight of good religion."[120]

How do we acknowledge the harm of religion? Logan offers one helpful route: Historians of religion, she suggests, can and should do the work of historically tracing specific ritual practices when they are designed to cause harm. In the case of Synanon, she argues, it is legitimate to designate it and its offshoots as a cult because it is possible to clearly locate the origins of its practices in military resocialization exercises that were created in order to break the personality down.

Logan's work is invaluable in historically tracing a specific type of harm and abuse that has occurred in new religious movements. However, much abuse and harm that occurs in religious contexts—minority and majority—is not traceable to nonreligious origins (such as military resocialization exercises) but rather, as Orsi emphasizes, is interwoven with religious authorities, power, institutions, cultures, beliefs, practices, and relationships. To clearly name, untangle, and counter these intersecting conditions that enable and perpetuate harm necessitates a multidisciplinary approach, one that critically and selectively draws on the multiple discourses available, including the wide range of frameworks and resources that fall under the broad category of "cult discourse."

To do this requires moving beyond what Benjamin Zablocki and Thomas Robbins named as the "divisive polarization" between the fields of NRM and cultic studies. In their 2001 edited collection *Misunderstanding Cults: Searching for Objectivity in a Controversial Field*, Zablocki and Robbins lament that the hostile relationship between the two camps had "plagued the academic study of religious movements" and "impeded learning and added confusion rather than clarity to a class of phenomena already beset with more than its share of confusion and misunderstanding."[121] Some individual religious studies scholars, such as Phillip C. Lucas, have attempted to bridge the divide by presenting and publishing on the topic of spiritual harm in NRMs in cultic studies venues.[122] Sociologist of religion and founder of Inform

Eileen Barker has also modelled and advocated for more dialogue between the two fields.[123]

As the 2021 AAR panel shows, however, the polarization between NRM scholarship and cultic studies continues to the present day and has undoubtedly come at a significant cost to victim-survivors of abuse in NRMs. Ashcraft, for instance, has acknowledged that NRM scholars could learn from cultic studies scholars' deeper understanding of different forms of violence within NRMs.[124] Thomas and Graham-Hyde have also called on scholars to engage more with cult discourse, sharing that while they might not always agree with podcast host Kacey Baker of *The Cult Vault*, their engagement with her work has enriched their scholarship.[125] Reflecting on her own research findings on abuse in NRMs, Harvey also emphasizes the importance of building bridges between NRM and cultic studies as well as between those researching abuse in religious and nonreligious contexts.[126]

One model for the type of needed multidisciplinary approach to abuse in NRMs was the Spiritual Abuse: Coercive Control in Religions conference held at the University of Chester in the United Kingdom on September 3–4, 2021. The conference was jointly hosted by the Department of Psychology and the Department of Theology and Religious Studies. It was co-organized by Lisa Oakley, professor of psychology; Wendy Dossett, professor emerita of religious studies; and Dawn Llewellyn, associate professor of religion and gender.[127] It is notable that two of the three organizers are feminist scholars of religion, and Llewellyn also served as chair of Chester Sexual Abuse Support Service. Reflecting on the interdisciplinary nature of the conference, Oakley explained that there was a "need to bring together people with different lenses on the topic to build a deeper awareness and mutual understanding. There is often little dialogue between disciplines, and it was essential that [the

Departments of] Psychology and Theology and Religious Studies came together to explore this topic."[128]

The conference's call for papers stated, "The term 'Spiritual Abuse" has increasingly been used to name the phenomenon of abuse, coercion and control within religious and spiritual traditions and contexts."[129] Conference presenters were remarkably diverse, including academics, survivors, religious leaders, lawyers, counselling psychologists, and policy and research analysts from around the world. These participants—several of whom, including Matthew Remski, Amelia Wood, Sarah Harvey, and Suzanne Newcombe, have been previously discussed in this book—examined abuse occurring in majority and minority religions, spiritual traditions, and wellness cultures across global contexts. Other presenters advocated for populations who have been ignored and delegitimated in consensus scholarship on abuse in NRMs, such as ex-members or "apostates" from groups like Scientology, Jehovah's Witnesses, and the New Kadampa Tradition (NKT). Most significantly, the conference was survivor-centered, employing a variety of strategies to support survivors' participation, including making available trained support workers from Replenished Life, an organization that supports people who have experienced abuse and trauma within religious contexts.

In her reflection on the conference, Dossett pushed religious studies scholars to consider what was at stake in the study of spiritual abuse. In her words, "The issue of spiritual abuse really throws into sharp relief, perhaps more than any other issue, questions around what it means to take an ethical stance as a religious studies scholar. This is not arm's length ethnography. There is a real risk here of my academic discipline ending up complicit in abuse by failing to call it out because of an academic fear around 'getting hands dirty'."[130]

Dossett's concern around the potential complicity of religious studies in abuse in religious settings had, in fact, been proven justified by Tenzin Peljor's complaint—discussed at the start of this book—that academics had ignored the "plight" of survivors because "our stories and what we have experienced has been [too] dirty to deal with in the 'pure' 'academic world.'"[131] It seems appropriate to have concluded this book with the ethical challenges raised by both survivors and feminist scholars of religion to treat survivors of abuse in religious contexts with the epistemological respect they have too often been denied in the study of new religious movements.

NOTES

CHAPTER 1. "I KNOW IT'S A POLITICALLY INCORRECT TERM, BUT I WAS IN A CULT"

1. Justin Whitaker, " A difficult but necessary read on the Shambhala organization . . . ," Facebook, September 11, 2024, https://www.facebook.com/justinswhitaker/posts/pfbidocr9ULeZa5YnrEEmrdj15myfSjZCnFew9quQpwXvWiF53HMDbHYCqZYTh2jGaMoXVl.

2. Be Scofield, "Secrets of Shambhala: In Pema Chodron's Shadow," *The Guru*, August 27, 2024, https://www.gurumag.com/pema-chodron-shambhala-cult/.

3. Robert Mayer, September 12, 2024, comment on Whitaker, "A difficult but necessary read on the Shambhala organization."

4. Allya Francesca Canepa, September 12, 2024, comment on Whitaker, "A difficult but necessary read on the Shambhala organization."

5. Justin Whitaker, September 12, 2024, comment on Whitaker, "A difficult but necessary read on the Shambhala organization."

6. Tenzin Peljor, *Tibetan Buddhism—Struggling with Diffi-Cult Issues* (blog), https://buddhism-controversy-blog.com/. For examples of articles see Tenpel, "Walking Free from Coercive, Cultic and Spiritual Abuse," July 28, 2023, https://buddhism-controversy-blog.com/2023/07/28/walking-free-from-coercive-cultic-and-spiritual-abuse/, and Nina Drew, "Cultic Experiences: The Untold Consequences and How to Find Healing," January 11, 2024, https://buddhism-controversy-blog.com/2024/01/11/cultic-experiences-the-untold-consequences-and-how-to-find-healing/.

7. Tenzin Peljor, September 13, 2024, comment on Whitaker, "A difficult but necessary read on the Shambhala organization."

8. Kevin Knox, September 13, 2024, comment on Whitaker, "A difficult but necessary read on the Shambhala organization."

9. Robert Mayer, September 13, 2024, comment on Whitaker, "A difficult but necessary read on the Shambhala organization."

10. See, for example, Mark Dunlop, "Why are Cults So Difficult to Oppose?," *Tibetan Buddhism—Struggling with Diffi-Cult Issues* (blog), August 1, 2018, https://buddhism-controversy-blog.com/2018/08/01/why-are-cults-so-difficult-to-oppose/.

11. Ann Gleig, September 12, 2024, comment on Whitaker, "A difficult but necessary read on the Shambhala organization."

12. Ann Gleig and Amy Langenberg, untitled book (Yale University Press, under advance contract).

13. For details of our survivor-centered approach and how it responds to a lacuna in Buddhist studies, see Ann Gleig and Amy Paris Langenberg, "Listening *for* and *to* Survivors of Sexual Abuse and Misconduct in Buddhism," *Religion* 55, no. 4 (August 3, 2025): 783–806; Ann Gleig and Amy Paris Langenberg, "Sexual Misconduct and Buddhism—Centering Survivors," *The Shiloh Project* (blog), November 18, 2020, https://shilohproject.blog/sexual-misconduct-and-buddhism-centering-survivors/.

14. The original website for the Abuse in Religious Contexts project is here: https://research.kent.ac.uk/airs/. An updated website can be found here: https://blogs.ed.ac.uk/airc/about-the-project/.

15. "About the Project," Abuse in Religious Contexts, accessed November 5, 2025, https://blogs.ed.ac.uk/airc/about-the-project/. I would like to credit and thank Sarah Harvey, a team member on the project, for the inspiration to use this definition of abuse. I decided to adopt the project's definition of abuse after reviewing Harvey's urgently needed book *Abuse in New Religious Movements* (Cambridge University Press, 2025).

16. W. Michael Ashcraft, *A Historical Introduction to the Study of New Religious Movements* (Routledge, 2018), 3. Ashcraft also notes another theory: that it came from Harold Turner, who he claims opened the Centre for the Study of New Religious Movements at Lancaster University in the United Kingdom. But this center was actually at the University of Aberdeen. See "The Harold Turner Collection," University of Birmingham, https://calmview.bham.ac.uk/Record.aspx?src=Catalog&id=XHT.

17. Ashcraft, *A Historical Introduction*, 4.

18. Aled Thomas and Edward Graham-Hyde, eds., *"Cult" Rhetoric in the 21st Century: Deconstructing the Study of New Religious Movements* (Bloomsbury Publishing, 2024), 14. The term "high demand group" has also been adopted as a more formal, less colloquial term by those critical of such groups.

For a critique of this term by an NRM scholar, see Joseph P. Laycock, "A Cult by Any Other Name: Is 'High Demand Group' a Useful Category?," *Nova Religio: The Journal of Alternative and Emergent Religions* 28, no. 1 (August, 2024): 90–104.

19. Ashcraft, *A Historical Introduction*, 104.

20. Ashcraft, 105. See also International Cultic Studies Association, https://www.icsahome.com/.

21. Ashcraft, *A Historical Introduction*, 8.

22. Ashcraft, 116–27.

23. Steven Hassan, "Cult Expert Steven Hassan's Freedom of Mind Resource Center," Freedom of Mind Resource Center, accessed November 5, 2025, https://freedomofmind.com, and Janja Lalich, "About Dr. Lalich," Lalich Center on Cults and Coercion, accessed May 7, 2025, https://www.lalichcenter.org/.

24. Alexandra Stein, *Terror, Love, and Brainwashing: Attachment in Cults and Totalitarian Systems* (Routledge, 2016); Daniel Shaw, *Traumatic Narcissism: Relational Systems of Subjugation* (New York: Routledge, 2013).

25. Michael Langone, *Recovery from Cults: Help for Victims of Psychological and Spiritual Abuse* (W.W. Norton and Company, 1995).

26. Lisa Oakley and Justin Humphreys, *Escaping the Maze of Spiritual Abuse: Creating Healthy Christian Cultures* (SPCK Publishing, 2019).

27. On gaslighting, see Paige L. Sweet, "The Sociology of Gaslighting," *American Sociological Review* 84, no. 5 (2019): 851–75, and Kate Manne, *Entitled: How Male Privilege Hurts Women* (Crown, 2020).

28. Evan Stark, *Coercive Control: How Men Entrap Women in Personal Life* (Oxford University Press, 2007), 23.

29. "Controlling or Coercive Behaviour in an Intimate or Family Relationship," last modified February 7, 2025, The Crown Prosecution Service, https://www.cps.gov.uk/legal-guidance/controlling-or-coercive-behaviour-intimate-or-family-relationship.

30. "What Is Coercive Control?," Women's Aid, accessed November 5, 2025, https://www.womensaid.org.uk/information-support/what-is-domestic-abuse/coercive-control/. For a full list of behaviors associated with coercive control, see "Controlling or Coercive Behaviour in an Intimate or Family Relationship," The Crown Prosecution Service, February 7, 2025, https://www.cps.gov.uk/prosecution-guidance/controlling-or-coercive-behaviour-intimate-or-family-relationship.

31. Roderick P. Dubrow-Marshall, "The Recognition of Cults," in *"Cult"*

Rhetoric, 96–112: 106. Dubrow-Marshall argues that cult discourse functions as a way to call out systemic abuse and coercion in groups, parallel to the way that terms such as "domestic abuse" or "rape culture" function to call out the systemic abuse and coercion of victims of sexual abuse or gender violence (106–7).

32. For full definitions, see Jennifer J. Freyd, "What Is DARVO?," Jennifer Joy Freyd, PhD, https://www.jjfreyd.com/darvo and Jennifer J. Freyd, "Institutional Betrayal and Institutional Courage," University of Oregon, https://dynamic.uoregon.edu/jjf/institutionalbetrayal/.

33. See *IndoctriNation*, https://podcasts.apple.com/us/podcast/indoctrination/id1373939526; *A Little Bit Culty*, https://alittlebitculty.com/; and *The Cult Vault*, https://www.cultvaultpodcast.com/.

34. Matthew Remski, *Practice and All Is Coming: Abuse, Cult Dynamics, and Healing in Yoga and Beyond* (Embodied Wisdom Publishing, 2019).

35. Derek Beres, Matthew Remski, and Julian Walker, "About," Conspirituality, accessed November 5, 2025, https://www.conspirituality.net/about.

36. My use of the term "disciplinary consensus" here is aligned with Benjamin Beit-Hallahmi's concept of "operative consensus" in his article "'O Truant Muse': Collaborationism and Research Integrity," in *Misunderstanding Cults: Searching for Objectivity in a Controversial Field*, ed. Benjamin Zablocki and Tom Robbins (University of Toronto Press, 2001): 35–70. It also aligns with Susannah Crockford's identification of a consensus view in NRM scholarship regarding cult rhetoric that she also challenges, in "'There is no QAnon': Cult Accusations in Contemporary American Political and Online Discourse," in *"Cult" Rhetoric*, 154–77.

37. "Cult," *Oxford English Dictionary*, https://www.oed.com/dictionary/cult_n. For a more detailed history of the term "cult," see Ashcraft, *A Historical Introduction*, 2–3.

38. Ashcraft, *A Historical Introduction*, 3.

39. Sean McCloud, *Making the American Religious Fringe: Exotics, Subversives, and Journalists, 1955–1993* (University of North Carolina Press, 2004).

40. McCloud, 55–94.

41. See Lorne L. Dawson, "Church-Sect-Cult: Constructing Typologies of Religious Groups," in *The Oxford Handbook of the Sociology of Religion*, ed. Peter B. Clarke (Oxford University Press, 2009), 525–44.

42. William Sims Bainbridge and Rodney Stark, "*Cult Formation: Three Compatible Models*," *Sociological Analysis* 40, no. 4 (Winter, 1979): 283–95.

43. Andrew Hartman, *A War for the Soul of America: A History of the Culture Wars*, 2nd ed. (University of Chicago Press, 2019), 10.

44. Hartman identifies the countercultural embrace of Asian religions such as Buddhism as a major liberal threat to the Christian Right.

45. Quoted in McCloud, *Making the American Religious Fringe*, 100.

46. McCloud, *Making the American Religious Fringe*, 100.

47. For a detailed history of this countercult lineage, see Ashcraft, *A Historical Introduction*, 33–37. He notes that J. Gordon Melton dates the lineage to William C. Irvine's 1917 publication of *Timely Warnings*, reprinted as William C. Irvine, *Heresies Exposed: A Brief Critical Examination in the Light of the Holy Scriptures of Some of the Prevailing Heresies and False Teachings of Today*, 11th ed. (Loizeaux Brothers, Bible Truth Depot, 1940). See also Douglas E. Cowan, *The Christian Countercult Movement* (Cambridge University Press, 2023).

48. Walter Martin, *The Kingdom of the Cults*, 6th ed. (Bethany House Publisher, 2019). Originally published in 1965.

49. Ashcraft, *A Historical Introduction*, 36.

50. McCloud, *Making the American Religious Fringe*, 122. As McCloud continues, by the late 1970s a loosely organized national coalition of parents, pastors, and psychiatrists who lobbied against cults had formed.

51. For a detailed account of the brainwashing narrative, see Ashcraft, *A Historical Introduction*, 105–26.

52. Margaret Thaler Singer and Janja Lalich, *Cults in Our Midst: The Hidden Menace in Our Everyday Lives* (Jossey-Bass, 1995).

53. For more information on Patrick, see Ashcraft, *A Historical Introduction*, 111–12.

54. Margaret Thaler Singer, "Therapy with Ex-Cult Members," *Journal of the National Association of Private Psychiatric Hospitals* 9, no. 4 (1978): 14–18.

55. Carol Giambalvo et al., "Changes in the North American Cult Awareness Movement," International Cultic Studies Association, 2013, https://articles1.icsahome.com/articles/changes-in-the-north-american-cult-awareness-movement.

56. Giambalvo et al., "Changes," n.p.

57. Giambalvo et al. date the start of the move away from this simplistic narrative to Steven Hassan's book *Combating Cult Mind Control* (Freedom of Mind Press, 1988); Giambalvo et al., "Changes," n.p.

58. Giambalvo et al., "Changes," n.p.

59. McCloud, *Making the American Religious Fringe*, 153–59.

60. Giambalvo et al., "Changes," n.p.

61. Ashcraft, *A Historical Introduction*, n.p.

62. David G. Bromley and Anson D. Shupe, *Strange Gods: The Great American Cult Scare* (Beacon Press, 1981), 1–2.

63. Bromley and Shupe, 16

64. Bromley and Shupe, 199.

65. Bromley and Shupe, 213.

66. Bromley and Shupe, 67.

67. James D. Tabor and Eugene V. Gallagher, *Why Waco? Cults and the Battle for Religious Freedom in America* (University of California Press, 1995); Catherine Wessinger, "Cult is an Inaccurate, Unhelpful and Dangerous Label for Followers of Trump, QAnon, and 1/6," *Religion Dispatches*, July 19, 2021, https://religiondispatches.org/cult-is-an-inaccurate-unhelpful-and-dangerous-label-for-followers-of-trump-qanon-and-1-6/.

68. CAM activists tend to view scholars as "cult apologists." While there are exceptions, the relationship between cultic studies figures and RM scholars has been an oppositional and hostile one. See Eileen Barker, "Religious Movements: Cult and Anticult Since Jonestown," *Annual Review of Sociology* 12, no. 1 (November, 1986): 329–46.

69. Ashcraft also agrees that "the narrative set by Bromley and Shupe was accepted by most scholars." Ashcraft, *A Historical Introduction*, 138.

70. David G. Bromley et al., "Atrocity Tales, the Unification Church, and the Social Construction of Evil," *Journal of Communication* 29, no. 3 (1979): 42–43.

71. Bromley et al., 44.

72. Bromley et al., 49.

73. Bromley et al., 50.

74. Bryan R. Wilson, "Apostates and New Religious Movements," Scientology, December 3, 1994, https://www.scientologyreligion.org/religious-expertises/apostates-and-new-religious-movements/.

75. Bryan R. Wilson, "Apostates and New Religious Movements," *STAND: Scientologists Taking Action Against Discrimination*, December 3, 1994, https://www.standleague.org/resources/expert-studies/apostates-and-new-religious-movements.html.

76. George D. Chryssides, "A History of Anti-Cult Rhetoric," in *"Cult" Rhetoric*, 40–46.

77. Phillip C. Lucas, "Foreword," in Erin Prophet, *Prophet's Daughter: My*

Life with Elizabeth Clare Prophet Inside the Church Universal and Triumphant (Lyons Press, 2008).

78. For a fascinating discussion of the methodological challenges of researching Scientology, see Aled J. Ll. Thomas, "Engaging with the Church of Scientology and the Free Zone in the Field: Challenges, Barriers, and Methods," *International Journal for the Study of New Religions* 10, no. 2 (2019): 121–37.

79. Benjamin E. Zeller, "Cult," in *Contested Concepts in the Study of Religion: A Critical Exploration*, ed. George D. Chryssides and Amy R. Whitehead (Bloomsbury, 2022), 27–31.

80. Richard Kent Evans, *MOVE: An American Religion* (Oxford University Press, 2020).

81. Eileen Barker, "Watching for Violence: A Comparative Analysis of the Roles of Five Types of Cult-Watching Groups," in *Cults, Religion, and Violence*, ed. David G. Bromley and J. Gordon Melton (Cambridge University Press, 2002), 123–48.

82. For an excellent analysis of the Satanic Panic, see Megan Goodwin, *Abusing Religion: Literary Persecution, Sex Scandals, and American Minority Religions* (Rutgers University Press, 2020). In general, however, Goodwin adopts the consensus approach to abuse in NRMs.

83. Catherine Wessinger, "'Culting': From Waco to Fundamentalist Mormons," *Religion Dispatches*, July 3, 2009, https://religiondispatches.org/culting-from-waco-to-fundamentalist-mormons/. See also Catherine Wessinger, "The Deaths of 76 Branch Davidians in April 1993 Could Have Been Avoided—So Why Didn't Anyone Care?," *The Conversation*, April 13, 2018, https://theconversation.com/the-deaths-of-76-branch-davidians-in-april-1993-could-have-been-avoided-so-why-didnt-anyone-care-90816.

84. Catherine Wessinger, "'Culting.'"

85. Pamela Saharah Dyson, *Premka: White Bird in a Golden Cage: My Life with Yogi Bhajan* (Eyes Wide Publishing, 2020).

86. Philip Deslippe and Stacie Stukin, "Yogi Bhajan, Yoga Guru and Founder of 3HO, 'More Likely Than Not' Sexually Abused Followers, Says Report," *Religious Studies News*, August 18, 2020, https://religionnews.com/2020/08/18/yogi-bhajan-yoga-guru-and-founder-of-3ho-more-likely-than-not-sexually-abused-followers-says-report/.

87. "IHRP Closure Statement" (public statement, July 28, 2025), https://drive.google.com/file/d/1gKjEGoVYP_DUtTYH_k4ZgVsldyJpD6Inview.

88. Philip Deslippe and Stacie Stukin, "3HO's Boarding Schools Were

a Living Hell," *Baaz*, May 27, 2024, https://www.baaznews.org/p/3hos-boarding-schools-abuse-yogi-bhajan.

89. Barbara Speed, "The Rise and Fall of the British Cult that Hid in Plain Sight," *The Guardian*, 24 July 2025, https://www.theguardian.com/news/2025/jul/24/jesus-army-fellowship-cult-noel-stanton.

90. The first monograph on abuse in NRMs—Sarah Harvey's *Abuse in New Religious Movements* was published by Cambridge University Press in December 2025. Notably, Harvey's research was part of the survivor-centered Abuse in Religious Contexts project.

91. "Hare Krishnas Lift the Lid on History of Child Abuse," *Religion News Service*, October 8, 1998, https://religionnews.com/1998/10/08/news-story-hare-krishnas-lift-the-lid-on-history-of-child-abuse/.

92. "ISKCON Abuse Cases Settled for USD 9.5 million," Pluralism Project Archive, Harvard University, May 24, 2005, https://hwpi.harvard.edu/pluralismarchive/news/iskcon-abuse-cases-settled-usd-95-million.

93. Beit-Hallahmi, "'O Truant Muse,'" 35–70. For a more detailed account of this episode, see Benjamin Beit-Hallahmi, *Academic Advocacy for New Religious Movements: Of Apocalypse and Justice* (Palgrave MacMillan, 2025), 1–9.

94. Ashcraft, *A Historical Introduction*, 177.

95. Ashcraft, 178.

96. Stephen A. Kent and Theresa Krebs, "Academic Compromise in the Social Scientific Study of Alternative Religions," *Nova Religio: The Journal of Alternative and Emergent Religions* 2, no. 1 (October 1998): 44–54.

97. Kent and Krebs, 44.

98. Kent and Krebs, 45.

99. Kent and Krebs, 45.

100. Kent and Krebs, "Academic Compromise," 49.

101. Beit-Hallahmi, "'O Truant Muse,'" 37.

102. Beit-Hallahmi, 37.

103. Beit-Hallahmi, 45.

104. Beit-Hallahmi, 45. Beit-Hallahmi has recently expanded on his argument; see Beit-Hallahmi, *Academic Advocacy*.

105. See Robert W. Balch, "Charisma and Corruption in the Love Family: Toward a Theory of Corruption in Charismatic Cults," in *Sex, Lies, and Sanctity: Religion and Deviance in Contemporary North America*, volume 5, ed. Mary Jo Neitz and Marion S. Goldman (JAI Press, 1995), 155–79, and James V. Spickard, "When None Dare Call It Evil: A Sociological Framework for Evaluating Abuse in Religions," in Neitz and Goldman, *Sex, Lies, and Sanc-*

tity, 251–68, which focus on the problem of abuse in NRMs. Another notable contribution is by Nancy Nason-Clark, "Conservative Protestants and Violence Against Women: Exploring the Rhetoric and the Response," in Neitz and Goldman, *Sex, Lies, and Sanctity*, 109–30. Here, Nason-Clark tackles the role Evangelical doctrine plays in domestic abuse in Protestant communities. She provides a structural framework that offers much to NRM scholars interested in analyzing abuse in NRMs.

106. Balch, "Charisma and Corruption," 177.

107. Balch, 178.

108. Emily Culpepper, "The Spiritual Movement of Radical Feminist Consciousness," in *Understanding the New Religions*, ed. Jacob Needleman and George Baker (Seabury Press, 1978), 220–34.

109. Culpepper, 221.

110. Culpepper, 221. She called on women to explore, rather than this pseudo-newness, a radical pre-patriarchal spiritual feminist consciousness.

111. Notably, Ashcraft also recognizes Jacobs's unique contributions to naming gendered forms of violence in NRMs. Ashcraft, *A Historical Introduction*, 177.

112. Janet Liebman Jacobs, *Divine Disenchantment: Deconverting from New Religions* (Indiana University Press, 1989).

113. Jacobs. See also Marion S. Goldman, *Passionate Journeys: Why Successful Women Joined a Cult* (University of Michigan Press, 1999).

114. Janet Liebman Jacobs, "Charisma, Male Entitlement, and the Abuse of Power," in *Bad Pastors: Clergy Misconduct in Modern America*, ed. Anson D. Shupe et al. (New York University Press, 2000), 113–30. The collection considers how abuse arises out of "organizational structures" across traditions and highlights similarities with other forms of abuse such as domestic violence.

115. Jacobs, "Charisma." Also notable is that Jacobs draws on Judith Herman, a therapist who has been at the forefront of survivor-centered approaches to sexual abuse. See Judith Herman, *Truth and Repair: How Trauma Survivors Envision Justice* (Basic Books, 2023).

116. Janet Liebman Jacobs, "Abuse in New Religious Movements: Challenges for the Sociology of Religion," in *Teaching New Religious Movements*, ed. David G. Bromley (Oxford University Press, 2007), 235.

117. Jacobs, 235.

118. Mary Jo Neitz, "Insiders, Outsiders, Advocates and Apostates and the Religions They Study: Location and the Sociology of Religion," *Critical Research on Religion* 1, no. 2 (2013): 129–40.

119. Email correspondence with Marion S. Goldman on June 11, 2021.

120. Carrie Rentschler et al., *Survivor-Centred Research: Guidelines, Principles, and Resources*, 2022, McGill University Institute for Gender, Sexuality, and Feminist Studies, 6, https://www.mcgill.ca/definetheline/files/definetheline/survivor-centred_research_rentschler_et_al._2022.pdf.

121. Gleig and Langenberg, "Listening *for* and *to* Survivors."

122. Gleig and Langenberg, 784.

123. Sara Ahmed, *Complaint!* (Duke University Press, 2021).

124. Ahmed, 4.

125. Gleig and Langenberg, "Listening *for* and *to* Survivors," 784.

CHAPTER 2. "WE CAN'T FIX SOMETHING IF WE CAN'T NAME IT"

1. Zoom conversation with Nancy Floy on June 24, 2022.

2. See "Survivors Program: Connecting Survivors of Guru and Teacher Abuse," Heartwood Center, accessed November 16, 2025, https://www.heartwoodcenter.com/meditation/survivors-program/.

3. See *IndoctriNation*, https://podcasts.apple.com/us/podcast/indoctrination/id1373939526.

4. "2023–24 U.S. Religious Landscape Study Interactive Database: Buddhists," Pew Research Center, 2025, https://www.pewresearch.org/religious-landscape-study/religious-tradition/buddhist/.

5. See, for example, Duncan Ryūken Williams, *American Sutra: A Story of Faith and Freedom in the Second World War* (Harvard University Press, 2019); Chenxing Han, *Be the Refuge: Raising the Voices of Asian American Buddhists* (North Atlantic Books, 2021); Scott A. Mitchell, *The Making of American Buddhism* (Oxford University Press, 2023).

6. For a discussion of the academic terminology used to describe these communities, see Ann Gleig, *American Dharma: Buddhism Beyond Modernity* (Yale University Press, 2019), 34–37.

7. Practitioners of color have challenged the whiteness of these communities and increased racial diversity and inclusivity, as well as crafting new forms of Buddhist community and practice. See, for example, Rima Vesely-Flad, *Black Buddhists and the Black Radical Tradition: The Practice of Stillness in the Movement for Liberation* (New York University Press, 2022); Ann Gleig, "Identities I: Race and Whiteness in American Buddhism," in *The Oxford*

Handbook of American Buddhism, ed. Ann Gleig and Scott A. Mitchell (Oxford University Press, 2024), 54–73.

8. For an excellent early account of the first wave of allegations and cases, see Katy Butler, "Events Are the Teacher: Working Through the Crisis at San Francisco Zen Center," *Coevolution Quarterly*, (Winter 1983), http://www.katybutler.com/author/articles/events-are-the-teacher-working-through-the-crisis-at-san-francisco-zen-center/, and Katy Butler, "Encountering the Shadow in Buddhist America," *Common Boundary Magazine* (May/June, 1990), http://www.katybutler.com/author/articles/encountering-the-shadow-in-buddhist-america/.

9. Michael Downing, *Shoes Outside the Door: Desire, Devotion, and Excess at San Francisco Zen Center* (Counterpoint Press), 2001.

10. For an account of this crisis, see Stephen Butterfield, *The Double Mirror: A Skeptical Journey into Buddhist Tantra* (North Atlantic Books, 1994).

11. Mick Brown, "The Precious One," *Telegraph Magazine*, February 2, 1995, 20–28.

12. Mark Oppenheimer, "Sex Scandal Has U.S. Buddhists Looking Within," *The New York Times*, August 20, 2010, https://www.nytimes.com/2010/08/21/us/21beliefs.html.

13. Corina Knoll, "Sex Abuse Allegations Surround L.A. Buddhist Teacher," *Los Angeles Times*, February 12, 2013, https://www.latimes.com/local/la-xpm-2013-feb-12-la-me-zen-master-20130213-story.html; Paul Vitello, "Joshu Sasaki, 107, Tainted Zen Master," *The New York Times*, August 4, 2014, https://www.nytimes.com/2014/08/05/us/joshu-sasaki-a-zen-master-tarnished-by-abuse-claims-dies-at-107.html.

14. A copy of the letter is available here: "Letter to Sogyal Lakar," Lion's Roar, July 14, 2017, https://www.lionsroar.com/wp-content/uploads/2017/07/Letter-to-Sogyal-Lakar-14-06-2017-.pdf.

15. Mary Finnegan and Rob Hogendoorn, *Sex and Violence in Tibetan Buddhism: The Rise and Fall of Sogyal Rinpoche* (Jorvik Press, 2019).

16. Andy Newman, "The 'King' of Shambhala Buddhism Is Undone by Abuse Report," *The New York Times*, July 11, 2018, https://www.nytimes.com/2018/07/11/nyregion/shambhala-sexual-misconduct.html.

17. "Buddhist Aberrations," International Cultic Studies Association, accessed November 17, 2025, https://www.icsahome.com/elibrary/topics/buddhist-aberrations, archived September 12, 2025, at the Wayback Machine.

18. Pseudonyms are used for all interviewees apart from Rachel Montgomery.

19. The racial demographics of the group reflect the historically dominant white demographics of meditation-based convert sanghas. There are a few people of color members of the Heartwood group, and Heartwood also runs a separate group for survivors of abuse in Buddhist contexts who identify as Black, Indigenous, or people of color (BIPOC), which is facilitated by an American therapist of South Asian descent. Two members of the Heartwood Advisory Board, both of whom are monastics and scholars—Dr. Choela Tenzin Dadon, who is Bhutanese, and Dr. Karma Tashi Choedron, who is Malaysian—provide support for survivors of abuse in Buddhist Asian contexts. My interview request was sent only to the main group because of my previous research with them. See the section "Who We Are" at "Survivors Program: Connecting Survivors of Guru and Teacher Abuse."

20. Gleig and Langenberg, untitled book.

21. Ann Gleig et al., "Reflection on Heartwood / Northwestern Symposium on Sexual Violence in Buddhism," *The Shiloh Project* (blog), November 4, 2024, https://shilohproject.blog/reflection-on-heartwood-symposium-on-sexual-violence-in-buddhism-centering-survivors-voices/.

22. Ruth Behar, *The Vulnerable Observer: Anthropology That Breaks Your Heart* (Beacon Press, 1997).

23. Nancy Scheper-Hughes, "The Primacy of the Ethical: Propositions for a Militant Anthropology," *Current Anthropology* 36, no. 3 (June 1, 1995): 409–40, https://escholarship.org/content/qt2xq430hc/qt2xq430hc.pdf.

24. Interview with Tess on February 1, 2025.

25. Interview with Rachel on January 29, 2025.

26. Interview with Betty on January 20, 2025.

27. Interview with Wongmo on January 22, 2025.

28. Interview with Darren on February 25, 2025.

29. Interview with Esther on February 21, 2025.

30. Tess interview.

31. Interview with Jo on January 17, 2025.

32. Interview with Molly on February 3, 2025.

33. Rachel Montgomery's story has been covered by a number of news sources. See, for instance, April Ehrlich, "Buddhist Center in Eugene Sued over Rape Accusation Against Master Guru," *Oregon Public Broadcasting*, April 20, 2023, https://www.klcc.org/crime-law-justice/2023-04-20/buddhist-center-in-eugene-sued-over-rape-accusation-against-master-guru. Montgomery filed a civil lawsuit against the Dzogchen Shri Singha organizations in Portland and Eugene, Oregon. In response to a request for an update on her

lawsuit, Montgomery and her lawyers shared that "the parties have reached a resolution of the case, the terms of which are confidential. We are putting this process behind us and moving forward." Personal communication with Carol Merchasin on October 27, 2025.

34. Rachel interview.

35. Esther interview.

36. Betty interview.

37. Tess interview.

38. Rachel interview.

39. See "Not Alone: A Conference for Survivors and Helping Professionals," SAFE Portland, https://www.safeportland.org/safe-conference.

40. Interview with Sandy on January 17, 2025.

41. Jo interview.

42. Alexandra Stein, *Terror, Love and Brainwashing: Attachment in Cults and Totalitarianism* (Routledge, 2016).

43. Darren interview.

44. See Matthew Remski, "Cultic Dynamics in Meditation Spaces," Cheetah House, https://courses.cheetahhouse.org/courses/cultic-dynamics-in-meditation-spaces.

45. Tess interview.

46. Tess interview.

47. Amanda Montell, *Cultish: The Language of Fanaticism* (Harper, 2021).

48. See Gillie Jenkinson, *Walking Free from the Trauma of Coercive, Cultic and Spiritual Abuse* (Routledge, 2023). Tenzin Peljor, another bridge figure between Buddhist and cultic studies, also highlights this book as particularly helpful. Tenpel, "Walking Free from Coercive, Cultic and Spiritual Abuse," July 28, 2023, *Tibetan Buddhism—Struggling with Diffi-Cult Issues* (blog), https://buddhism-controversy-blog.com/2023/07/28/walking-free-from-coercive-cultic-and-spiritual-abuse/.

49. Interview with Taylor on February 20, 2025.

50. See End Coercive Control USA, https://endcoercivecontrolusa.com/.

51. See Demaris Wehr, "Spiritual Abuse: When Good People Do Bad Things," in *The Psychology of Mature Spirituality: Integrity, Wisdom, Transcendence,* ed. Polly Young-Eisendrath and Melvin E. Miller (Brunner-Routledge, 2000), 37–48.

52. Interview with Riley on January 21, 2025.

53. Rachel interview.

54. Interview with Virginia on January 18, 2025.

55. Molly interview.

56. For a review of *Holy Hell*, see Noah Berlatsky, "Holy Hell and the Truth About Cults: 'They're Not Going to Give It Up Easily,'" *The Guardian*, May 27, 2016, https://www.theguardian.com/film/2016/may/27/holy-hell-documentary-truth-about-cults.

57. Rachel interview.

58. Jo interview.

59. Taylor interview.

60. Riley interview.

61. Betty interview.

62. Rachel interview.

63. Taylor interview.

64. Jo interview.

65. Rachel interview.

66. Betty interview.

67. Interview with Hannah on February 21, 2025.

68. Betty interview.

69. Sandy interview.

70. Molly interview.

71. Betty interview.

72. Rachel interview.

73. Virginia interview.

74. Sandy interview.

75. Hannah interview.

76. Personal correspondence with Hannah on February 21, 2025.

77. Personal writings shared by Hannah on February 21, 2025.

78. Tess interview.

79. Tess interview.

80. Tess interview.

81. Wongmo interview.

82. Wongmo interview.

83. Wongmo interview.

84. Riley interview.

85. Hannah interview.

86. Wongmo interview.

87. Wongmo interview.

88. Tess interview.

89. Darren interview.

90. Esther interview.

91. Molly interview.

92. Wongmo interview.

93. Hannah interview and personal correspondence.

94. Darren interview.

95. Hannah interview.

96. Betty interview.

97. Matthew Remski, *Surviving Modern Yoga: Cult Dynamics, Charismatic Leaders, and What Survivors Can Teach Us* (North Atlantic Books, 2024), xxv.

98. Remski, xliii.

99. Remski, 47.

100. Virginia interview. This view reflects nineteenth-century Protestant views of Vajrayana Buddhism as a degenerate form of the early Buddhism of the Pali Canon. See Samuel M. Grimes, "Why Is Newar Buddhism Largely Ignored in Buddhist Studies? Protestantism, the Narrative of Decline, and the Position of Invisibility," *Journal of the American Academy of Religion* 92, no. 4 (December 2024): 603–24.

101. The articles included Robert Mayer, "The Figure of Maheśvara/Rudra in the rÑiṅ-Ma-Pa Tantric Tradition," *Journal of the International Association of Buddhist Studies* 21, no. 2 (1998): 271–310; Haoran Hou, "The Ritual Use of Human Effigies in the Esoteric Buddhist Literature from Karakhoto," *BuddhistRoad Paper* 2.3 (2022): 1–24; and Holly Gayley, "Revisiting the 'Secret Consort' (*Gsang Yum*) in Tibetan Buddhism," *Religions* 9, no. 6 (2018): 179.

102. Christine A. Chandler, *Enthralled: The Guru Cult of Tibetan Buddhism*, 1st ed. (self-pub., CreateSpace, 2017).

103. Catalog copy of Chandler, *Enthralled.*

104. *Enthralled* has been discussed in at least three Reddit groups that focus on abuse in Buddhism, with the most substantial engagement found on r/ShambhalaBuddhism. On that discussion thread, a few participants express appreciation for certain dynamics Chandler pointed out; others, however, have labelled her claims as "lurid" and "implausible" and suggested they were part of a trauma response. For example, see KalajokiKachina, "Has Anyone Read ENTHRALLED by Christine A Chandler, Ex Shambhalian? If Not, You May Want To," Reddit, September 27, 2019, https://www.reddit.com/r/ShambhalaBuddhism/comments/da4hg3/has_anyone_read_enthralled_by_christine_a/.

105. David G. Bromley et al., "Atrocity Tales."

106. Leigh Gilmore, *Tainted Witness: Why We Doubt What Women Say About Their Lives* (Columbia University Press, 2017).

107. Gilmore 1.

108. Gilmore, 2.

109. Gilmore, 5.

110. Gilmore, 21.

111. Gilmore, 5–6.

112. Esther interview.

CHAPTER 3. FROM A "CAPITAL-C CULT" TO A "POTENTIALLY CULTISH CULTURE"

1. Julie Seido Nelson, "How to Choose a Sangha: A Writer and Zen Teacher on Discerning Healthy Buddhist Communities from Cultish Enterprises," *Tricycle: The Buddhist Review*, March 8, 2025, https://tricycle.org/article/how-to-choose-a-sangha/.

2. Nelson.

3. Julie Seido Nelson, *Practicing Safe Zen: Navigating the Pitfalls on the Road to Liberation* (Monkfish Book Publishing, 2025).

4. "About the Resilient Sangha Project," Greater Boston Zen Community, last modified November 15, 2023, https://bostonzen.org/resilientsangha/.

5. "A Potentially Cultish Culture," Greater Boston Zen Community, June 12, 2022, https://bostonzen.org/resilient-sangha/culture/.

6. "About the Resilient Sangha Project."

7. "Common Dynamics (DARVO)," Greater Boston Zen Community, June 12, 2022, https://bostonzen.org/resilient-sangha/DARVO/. "Why I Stayed: A Message from the Survivor," Greater Boston Zen Community, June 12, 2022, https://bostonzen.org/resilient-sangha/survivor/.

8. "Why I Stayed."

9. Thomas and Graham-Hyde, *"Cult" Rhetoric in the 21st Century: Deconstructing the Study of New Religious Movements.*

10. Aled Thomas and Edward Graham-Hyde, "'Cult' Rhetoric in the Twenty-First Century," in *"Cult" Rhetoric*, 3–20.

11. Thomas and Graham-Hyde, 4.

12. Thomas and Graham-Hyde, 9.

13. Thomas and Graham-Hyde, 9–10.

14. Thomas and Graham-Hyde, 10.

15. Suzanne Newcombe and Sarah Harvey, "Balancing Pragmatism and Precision: Inform's Approach to Cult Rhetoric," in *"Cult" Rhetoric*, 21–39.

16. Newcombe and Harvey, 34.

17. Newcombe and Harvey, 34.

18. Newcombe and Harvey, 33.

19. Newcombe and Harvey, 35.

20. Susannah Crockford, "'There Is No QAnon': Cult Accusations in Contemporary American Political and Online Discourse," in *"Cult" Rhetoric*, 154–77.

21. Crockford, 161.

22. Crockford, 161.

23. Crockford, 163.

24. Crockford, 164.

25. Crockford, 161.

26. Crockford, 168.

27. Crockford, 156.

28. Crockford, 156.

29. Dana Logan, "It Was Never About the Snakes: Synanon, Cult, and the Devil in Religious Studies," *Religion and American Culture* 33, no. 3 (2025): 283–319.

30. Logan, 293.

31. Logan, 291.

32. Rachel Aviv, "The Shadow Penal System for Struggling Kids," *The New Yorker*, October 11, 2021, https://www.newyorker.com/magazine/2021/10/18/the-shadow-penal-system-for-struggling-kids.

33. Aviv.

34. Logan, "It Was Never About the Snakes," 303.

35. Jonathan Z. Smith, *Imagining Religion: From Babylon to Jonestown* (Chicago University Press, 1982), 111.

36. Robert A. Orsi, *Between Heaven and Earth: The Religious Worlds People Make and the Scholars Who Study Them* (Princeton University Press, 2004), quoted in Logan, "It Was Never About the Snakes," 285.

37. Logan, "It Was Never About the Snakes," 285–86.

38. Logan, 308.

39. Logan, 287.

40. Logan notes, for instance, that "Megan Goodwin has argued that any designation of cult is tinged with a heteronormative, racist judgment." Logan, "It Was Never About the Snakes," 283.

41. Logan, 287.

42. Ashcraft, *A Historical Introduction*, 187–88.

43. Erin Prophet et al., "Round Table on Identifying, Naming and Treating Harm in New Religious Movements," WRSP—World Religions and Spirituality Project, July 14, 2022, video, 2:43:14, https://www.youtube.com/watch?v=9qp7muXPwoU.

44. Prophet et al., "Round Table."

45. Miranda Leitsinger, "#MeToo Unmasks the Open Secret of Sexual Abuse in Yoga," KQED, last modified July 16, 2024, https://www.kqed.org/news/11690316/metoo-unmasks-the-open-secret-of-sexual-abuse-in-yoga.

46. "Message from the Board of Directors of the Iyengar Yoga Association of Los Angeles," IYALA, August 23, 2019, https://iyila.org/message-from-the-board-of-directors-of-the-iyengar-yoga-association-of-los-angeles-2/.

47. Prophet et al., "Round Table."

48. Corina Knoll, "Sex Abuse Allegations Surround L.A. Buddhist Teacher," *Los Angeles Times*, February 12, 2013, https://www.latimes.com/local/la-xpm-2013-feb-12-la-me-zen-master-20130213-story.html; Mark Oppenheimer, "Sex Scandal Has U.S. Buddhists Looking Within," *The New York Times*, August 20, 2010, https://www.nytimes.com/2010/08/21/us/21beliefs.html; Jackson Barnett, "Shambhala, the Boulder-Born Buddhist Organization, Suppressed Allegations of Abuse, Ex-Members Say," *The Denver Post*, July 7, 2019, https://www.denverpost.com/2019/07/07/shambhala-sexual-abuse/; Andy Newman, "The 'King' of Shambhala Buddhism Is Undone by Abuse Report," *The New York Times*, July 11, 2018, https://www.nytimes.com/2018/07/11/nyregion/shambhala-sexual-misconduct.html; Wendy Biddlecombe Agsar, "Lawsuit Against Ezra Bayda and Zen Center San Diego Ends with Settlement," *Tricycle: The Buddhist Review*, June 28, 2022, https://tricycle.org/article/ezra-bayda-lawsuit/.

49. For a blistering critique of NRM scholars' treatment of the Children of God, including the murder-suicide of Ricky Rodriguez, see Beit-Hallahmi, *Academic Advocacy for New Religious Movements*, 43–76.

50. Steven Brocklehurst, "Children of God Cult was 'Hell on Earth,'" BBC, June 26, 2018, https://www.bbc.com/news/uk-scotland-44613932; Faith Jones, "'Sex Cult Nun' Says Discovering Self-Ownership Helped Her to Break Free from The Family," interview by Terry Gross, Fresh Air, WHYY, December 21, 2021, https://www.npr.org/2021/12/21/1065757559/sex-cult-nun-faith-jones. In a 1995 ruling, British judge Lord Justice Alan Ward found that the group had in the past engaged in abusive physical and sexual practices involving mi-

nors and required that the group denounce any of Berg's writings that were responsible for children in The Family having been subjected to physical or sexual abuse. He also found that by 1995 The Family had abandoned these practices and concluded that it was a safe environment for children. Alan Ward, "Judgement of Lord Justice Ward," ExFamily.org, accessed December 31, 2025, http://www.exfamily.org/art/misc/justward.htm.

51. "Former Aides to Guru in Oregon Plead Guilty to Numerous Crimes," *The New York Times*, July 23, 1986, https://www.nytimes.com/1986/07/23/us/former-aides-to-guru-in-oregon-plead-guilty-to-numerous-crimes.html.

52. See, for instance, Lily Dunn, *Sins of My Father: A Daughter, A Cult, A Wild Unravelling* (Weidenfeld & Nicolson, 2022) and the Rajneesh cult documentary *Children of the Cult*, dir. Maroesja Perizonius and Alice McShane (2024), https://www.dartmouthfilms.com/childrenofthecult.

53. Prophet et al., "Round Table."

54. Phil Williams, "'Take the Damn Filter Off.' Former Remnant Leader Says Church Needs to Admit Role in Child's Death," February 19, 2024, *NewsChannel 5 Investigates*, https://www.newschannel5.com/news/newschannel-5-investigates/take-the-damn-filter-off-former-remnant-leader-says-church-needs-to-admit-role-in-childs-death.

55. For coverage of the convictions following the raid on Zion, see James C. McKinley Jr., "Polygamist Sect Leader Convicted of Sexual Assault," *The New York Times*, November 5, 2009, https://www.nytimes.com/2009/11/06/us/06polygamy.html; John Dougherty and Kirk Johnson, "Sect Leader Is Convicted as an Accomplice to Rape," *The New York Times*, September 26, 2007, https://www.nytimes.com/2007/09/26/us/26jeffs.html; The Associated Press, "Texas: Polygamist Leader Gets Life Sentence," *The New York Times*, August 9, 2011, https://www.nytimes.com/2011/08/10/us/10brfs-POLYGAMISTLE_BRF.html. accessed December 31, 2025. For an overview of charges against the FLDS, see CNN Editorial Research, "Fundamentalist Church of Jesus Christ of Latter-Day Saints Fast Facts," *CNN US*, last modified December 29, 2025, https://www.cnn.com/us/fundamentalist-church-of-jesus-christ-of-latter-day-saints-fast-facts.

56. For more examples of the problematic consensus approach to abuse allegations in NRMs, which prioritizes mitigating harm against NRMs over the testimonies of alleged victim-survivors of abuse *within* NRMs, see coverage of the legal convictions against Korean pastor Jung Myung Seok and the pending court case against Gregorian Bivolaru, the Romanian founder of the MISA (Movement for Spiritual Integration into the Absolute) yoga school, such as

can be found on religious liberties and human rights magazine *Bitter Winter* at https://bitterwinter.org/. See also Massimo Introvigne, *Sacred Eroticism: Tantra and Eros in the Movement for Spiritual Integration into the Absolute (MISA)* (Mimesis International, 2024).

57. Sarah Harvey, *Abuse in New Religious Movements* (Cambridge University Press, 2025).

58. Harvey, 4.

59. Harvey, 5.

60. Harvey, 8–12.

61. Harvey, 13–16.

62. Harvey, 13.

63. Harvey, 56.

64. Harvey, 57.

65. Harvey, 57.

66. Brian Clites, "Breaking our Silence: A Primer for Research on Clergy Sexual Misconduct," Cushwa Center for the Study of American Catholicism, University of Notre Dame, November 16, 2020, https://cushwa.nd.edu/news/breaking-our-silence/.

67. Oakley and Humphreys, *Escaping the Maze of Spiritual Abuse*, 20.

68. Logan, "It Was Never About the Snakes," 308.

69. Logan, 283.

70. Harvey, *Abuse in New Religious Movements*, 52–53.

71. Harvey, 25.

72. Dubrow-Marshall, "The Recognition of Cults," in *"Cult" Rhetoric*, 96–112; 106–7.

73. Dubrow-Marshall, 107.

74. For an example of how feminist analyses of abuse are informing cult discourse, see Rachel Bernstein and Nicole Bedera, "On the Wrong Side w/ Nicole Bedera, Ph.D," January 15, 2025, in *IndoctriNation*, podcast, 1:24:35, https://podcasts.apple.com/us/podcast/on-the-wrong-side-w-nicole-bedera-ph-d/id1373939526?i=1000684088254. For a feminist-informed critique of cultic studies's treatment of coercive control, see Erin Martine Sessions and Bernard Doherty, "'Cults,' Coercion, and Control: Rhetoric, Reality, and the Return of 'Brainwashing'?," *Implicit Religion* 24, no. 2 (2023): 161–94.

75. Harvey, *Abuse in New Religious Movements*, 6.

76. Harvey, 12.

77. See, for instance, Oakley and Humphreys, *Escaping the Maze of Spiritual Abuse*.

78. Oakley and Humphreys, *Escaping the Maze of Spiritual Abuse*, 25.

79. Amelia Wood, "Spiritual and Sexual Abuse in Modern Yoga Contexts: Re-Defining Parameters as a Means to Resist Injustice" (conference paper, Religion & Sexual Abuse Project Conference, University of California, Riverside, March 4, 2022), https://www.academia.edu/104537881/Spiritual_and_Sexual_Abuse_in_Modern_Yoga_Contexts_Re_defining_Parameters_as_a_Means_to_Resist_Injustice.

80. Bernstein and Bedera, "On the Wrong Side w/Nicole Bedera"; Kacey Baker and Nicole Bedera, "S3 E3 How Universities Protect Perpetrators and Betray Survivors of Sexual Violence," June 10, 2024, in *The Cult Vault*, podcast, 1:19:36, https://podcasts.apple.com/gb/podcast/s3-e3-how-universities-protect-perpetrators-and/id1514656568?i=1000671914187.

81. Email correspondence with Nicole Bedera on April 14, 2025.

82. Lama Rod Owens et al., "Sexual Abuse, Whiteness, and Patriarchy," Ann Gleig, October 5, 2021, video, 1:27:51, https://www.youtube.com/watch?v=yDY6sgMIi9s.

83. For more information, see @SurvivingUniversalUK," Surviving Universal UK, accessed November 30, 2025, https://linktr.ee/survivinguniversaluk. See also Rachael Reign, "I Gave Years to the UCKG Evangelical Church Before Realising I Had to Escape Its Clutches," *The Guardian*, December 2, 2022, https://www.theguardian.com/commentisfree/2022/dec/02/uckg-evangelical-church-survivors; Sarah Edmondson et al., "Teenage Exorcisms & Mega-Church Millions: Rachael Reign's UCKG Story," July 14, 2025, *A Little Bit Culty*, podcast, 1:09:02, https://alittlebitculty.com/episode/teenage-exorcisms-mega-church-millions-rachael-reigns-uckg-story.

84. Alexander Barnes-Ross and Rachael Reign, "Surviving UCKG—Rachael Reign and the Universal Church of the Kingdom of God," April 1, 2025, in *Potential Trouble Source*, podcast, *1:22:38*, https://podcasts.apple.com/gb/podcast/surviving-uckg-rachael-reign-and-the-universal/id1735110600?i=1000701719963; "Breaking Free: Rachel Reign founder of Surviving Universal UK," Black British Parent, July 18, 2024, video, 1:22:38, https://www.youtube.com/watch?v=WQtbf9sw6NU.

85. Nikki G., "My Story: Certified Trauma Recovery Coach," Nikki G. Speaks, accessed November 30, 2025, https://www.nikkigspeaks.com/about.

86. "About Safer Sex-Positive & Spiritual Communities," 3SC Safer Sex-Positive & Spiritual Communities, accessed May 16, 2025, https://3sc.community/about/; Rachel Bernstein and Cara Cordoni, "Cult Hopping Chronicles Pt.1: A Journey Through Control and Liberation with Cara

Cordoni," April 30, 2024, *IndoctriNation*, podcast, 1:15:03, https://podcasts.apple.com/au/podcast/cult-hopping-chronicles-pt-1-a-journey-through/id1373939526?i=1000705543206.

87. For examples of works that show multiple uses of cult discourse approach, see Cody Musselman, "Drinking the Crossfit Kool-Aid: Cult Marketing Meets Functional Fitness," in *Selling the Sacred: Religion and Marketing from Crossfit to QAnon*, ed. Mara Einstein and Sarah McFarland Taylor (Routledge, 2024), 233–49; and Philip Deslippe, "Past the Pejorative: Understanding the Word 'Cult' Through Its Use in American Newspapers During the Nineties," *Implicit Religion* 24, no. 2 (2023): 195–217.

88. For a critique of Hassan, see "202: Steve Hassan and the Trans Cult Conspiracy Theory," April 18, 2024, in *Conspirituality*, podcast, 1:22:01, https://www.conspirituality.net/episodes/202-steve-hassan-trans-cult-conspiracy-theory.

89. Logan, "It Was Never About the Snakes," 285.

90. Logan, 285.

91. See Project Resist, https://www.projectresist.org.uk/.

92. Pragna Patel's extensive work on race, gender, and class justice is discussed in "On Sisters!: Pragna Patel & Meena Patel of Southall Black Sisters," April 7, 2025, in *Fruitmarket Segments*, podcast, 59:20, https://www.iheart.com/podcast/1323-fruitmarket-segments-217601419/episode/on-sisters-pragna-patel-meena-271909276/. For an example of her written work, see Pragna Patel, "The Sharia Debate in the UK: Who Will Listen to Our Voices?," *Open Democracy*, December 14, 2016, https://www.opendemocracy.net/en/5050/sharia-debate-who-will-listen-to-us/.

93. Pragna Patel, "Religious Abuse in South Asian Contexts" (conference paper, Apostasy Conference, Humanists UK, October 9, 2024), https://humanists.uk/events/apostasy-conference-2024/.

94. A similar argument was made at the conference by Yehudis Fletcher. See Yehudis Fletcher, "Replicating and Reiterating Harm: How UKState Policies Enable Abuse Within High-control Religions" (conference paper, Apostasy Conference, Humanists UK, October 9, 2024), https://humanists.uk/events/apostasy-conference-2024/.

95. Emma Park, "'We Need to Move from Identity Politics to a Politics of Solidarity'—Interview with Pragna Patel," *The Freethinker*, July 15, 2022 https://freethinker.co.uk/2022/07/interview-with-pragna-patel/.

96. Yehudis Fletcher, *Chutzpah: A Memoir of Faith, Sexuality and Daring to Stay* (Doubleday, 2025).

97. See Nahamu, https://nahamu.org/.

98. Yehudis Fletcher, "How 'Progressive' Feminists Are Failing Haredi Women," *Haaretz*, November 21, 2022, https://www.haaretz.com/jewish/2022-11-21/ty-article-opinion/.highlight/how-feminists-are-failing-haredi-women/00000184-91c8-d53f-a5fe-bbca33510000.

99. Fletcher.

100. Dyson, Premka: *White Bird in a Golden Cage.*

101. Email correspondence with Philip Deslippe on June 26, 2025.

102. Deslippe and Stukin, "3HO's Boarding Schools Were A Living Hell"; Philip Deslippe and Stacie Stukin, "Deslippe & Stukin: How 'Siri Singh Sahib' Yogi Bhajan Created An Empire," *Baaz*, July, 19, 2022, https://www.baaznews.org/p/yogi-bhajan-siri-singh-sahib-expose; Deslippe and Stukin, "Yogi Bhajan, Yoga Guru and Founder of 3HO, 'More Likely Than Not' Sexually Abused Followers, Says Report."

103. Deslippe correspondence.

104. "Religious Institutions," Royal Commission into Institutional Responses to Child Sexual Abuse, December 2017, https://www.childabuseroyalcommission.gov.au/religious-institutions.

105. "Religious Institutions."

106. "SNAP Applauds California Bill to Prohibit the Sexual Abuse of Adults by Clergy," SNAP Network, January 8, 2024, https://www.snapnetwork.org/snap_applauds_california_bill_to_prohibit_the_sexual_abuse_of_adults_by_clergy, archived February 2, 2024, at the Wayback Machine.

107. Diana Garland, "The Prevalence of Clergy Sexual Misconduct with Adults: A Research Study—Executive Summary," Diana R. Garland School of Social Work, Baylor University, (n.d.), accessed July 2, 2025, *https://socialwork.web.baylor.edu/executive-summary.*

108. David K. Pooler, "Preventing & Responding to Clergy Perpetrated Sexual Abuse: A Guide to Best Practices," Diana R. Garland School of Social Work, Baylor University, October 25, 2017, https://www.baylor.edu/social_work/doc.php/302534.pdf.

109. Aaron Weaver, "Clergy Sexual Abuse of Adults Causes Deep Trauma, Requires Urgent Reforms," June 12, 2025, Baptist History and Heritage Society, https://www.thebhhs.org/clergy-sexual-abuse-of-adults-causes-deep-trauma-requires-urgent-reforms/.

110. Gina Christian, "California Lawmaker Introduces Bill Tackling Clergy Sexual Abuse of Adults," *OSV News*, n.d., https://www.osvnews.com/california-lawmaker-introduces-bill-tackling-clergy-sexual-abuse-of-adults/.

111. Eliza Griswold, "Yoga Reconsiders the Role of the Guru in the Age of #MeToo," *The New Yorker*, July 23, 2019, https://www.newyorker.com/news/news-desk/yoga-reconsiders-the-role-of-the-guru-in-the-age-of-metoo; Adrian Horton, "'He Got Away with It'": How the Founder of Bikram Yoga Built an Empire on Abuse," *The Guardian*, November 20, 2019, https://www.theguardian.com/film/2019/nov/20/bikram-choudhury-yoga-founder-abuse-netflix-documentary; Edward Helmore, "'Shame and Betrayal': Sexual Abuse Within the Spiritual Healing Industry Comes to Light," *The Guardian*, May 26, 2024, https://www.theguardian.com/society/article/2024/may/26/sexual-abuse-spiritual-healing-industry.

112. Johanna Stiebert, ed., *Abuse in World Religions: Articulating the Problem* (Routledge, 2025).

113. Clites, "Breaking Our Silence"; Gleig and Langenberg, "Listening *for* and *to* Survivors."

114. Robert A. Orsi, "What Is Catholic About the Clergy Sex Abuse Crisis?," in *The Anthropology of Catholicism: A Reader*, ed. Kristin Norget, Valentina Napolitano, and Maya Mayblin (University of California Press, 2017), 282–92: 285.

115. Robert A. Orsi, "The Study of Religion on the Other Side of Disgust," *Harvard Divinity Bulletin*, Spring/Summer 2019, https://bulletin.hds.harvard.edu/the-study-of-religion-on-the-other-side-of-disgust/.

116. See Samah Choudhury and Juliane Hammer, eds., *Sexual Violence in Muslim Communities: Towards Awareness and Accountability*, OpenBU, Boston University Libraries, December 11, 2024, https://open.bu.edu/items/8b82e031-b23c-456b-8d8b-d26b670e0981.

117. Rose Deighton-Mohammed, "A Critical Approach to the Study of Religious and Sexual Abuse in Sufi Communities," in *Sexual Violence in Muslim Communities: Towards Awareness and Accountability*, ed. Samah Choudhury and Juliane Hammer (OpenBU, 2024), 210–20, 213. Notably, Deighton-Mohammed compares her survivor-centered approach with that of Megan Goodwin's approach to abuse in Goodwin's book *Abusing Religion*.

118. Harvey, *Abuse in New Religious Movements*, 3.

119. Orsi, *Between Heaven and Earth*.

120. Orsi, "The Study of Religion."

121. Robbins and Zablocki, *Misunderstanding Cults*, 3.

122. Phillip Charles Lucas, "Spiritual Harm in New Religions: Reflections on Interviews with Former Members of NRMs," *Cultic Stud-*

ies Review 2, no. 1 (2003): 30–37, https://articles2.icsahome.com/articles /spiritual-harm-in-new-religions-lucas.

123. Eileen Barker, "Harm and New Religious Movements (NRMs): Some Notes on a Sociological Perspective," *Cultic Studies Review* 2, no. 1 (2003), https://articles1.icsahome.com/articles/harm-and-new-religious-movements --nrms--some-notes-on-a-sociological-perspective; Eileen Barker, "From Cult Wars to Constructive Cooperation—Well, Sometimes," in *"Cult Wars" in Historical Perspective: New and Minority Religions*, ed. Eugene V. Gallagher (Routledge, 2017), 9–22.

124. Ashcraft, *A Historical Introduction*, 178.

125. Thomas and Graham-Hyde, *"Cult" Rhetoric*, 14.

126. Harvey, *Abuse in New Religious Movements*, 58.

127. See Dr. Lisa Oakley, https://www.chester.ac.uk/staff-directory /loakley/; Dr. Wendy Dossett, https://www.wedossett.com/; and Dr. Dawn Llewellyn, https://www.chester.ac.uk/staff-directory/dllewellyn/.

128. Lisa Oakley, "Reflection on the Conference" (conference paper, Spiritual Abuse: Coercive Control in Religions, University of Chester, September 3–4, 2021), URL no longer available.

129. Conference Call for Papers (call for papers, Spiritual Abuse: Coercive Control in Religions, University of Chester, September 4–5, 2020), https:// www.religiousstudiesproject.com/wp-content/uploads/2020/01/Spiritual -Abuse_Coercive-Control-in-Religions.pdf. Note that the conference date was later changed to September 3–4, 2021 because of the COVID-19 pandemic.

130. Wendy Dossett, "Reflections on the Spiritual Abuse Conference" (personal document shared with author on October 7, 2024).

131. Peljor, September 13, 2024, comment on Whitaker.

INDEX

GEORGE H. SHRIVER LECTURE SERIES IN RELIGION IN AMERICAN HISTORY

1 *Religion and the American Nation: Historiography and History*, by JOHN F. WILSON

2 *The Protestant Voice in American Pluralism*, by MARTIN E. MARTY

3 *The Creation-Evolution Debate: Historical Perspectives*, by EDWARD J. LARSON

4 *Religion Enters the Academy: The Origins of the Scholarly Study of Religion in America*, by JAMES TURNER

5 *The Faiths of the Postwar Presidents: From Truman to Obama*, by DAVID L. HOLMES

6 *Urban Origins of American Judaism*, by DEBORAH DASH MOORE

7 *Of Gods and Games: Religious Faith and Modern Sports*, by WILLIAM J. BAKER

8 *An Uncommon Faith: A Pragmatic Approach to the Study of African American Religion*, by EDDIE S. GLAUDE JR.

9 *Southern Religion in the World: Three Stories*, by PAUL HARVEY

10 *Appalachian Mountain Christianity: The Spirituality of Otherness*, by BILL J. LEONARD

11 *Talking About Cults: Abuse and the Study of New Religious Movements*, by ANN GLEIG

www.ingramcontent.com/pod-product-compliance
Lightning Source LLC
LaVergne TN
LVHW091658201026
850680LV00012B/115